COHLER ON DESIGN

COHLER ON DESIGN

Eric Cohler

THE MONACELLI PRESS

To my family. Without family there is no beginning and no future. No here and now.

How can we live without our lives?
How will we know it's us without our past?
—John Steinbeck, *The Grapes of Wrath*

Richard Ridge

CONTENTS

FOREWORD

I first met Eric Cohler some years ago at a dinner party at the home of cousins of mine who also happened to be clients of his. I had gone to the dinner with my usual anticipatory dread of social gatherings but quickly found myself caught up in delightful conversation with Eric, next to whom I had been seated. He struck me then as now as a real original—a mixture of an open, ever-curious boy and an opinionated, deeply sophisticated adult. I remember our talk ranging all over the place, from immediate matters to long-ago memories, stopping along the way to touch on books, film, art—and, if I recall correctly, our shared nostalgia for certain vanished Upper East Side landmarks, like the movie theater that once stood on Madison Avenue and Eighty-Fifth Street. Eric also got into a spirited discussion with my young daughter and I remember thinking how varied a frame of reference he had, one which included a fascination with things that might be thought childish by a stodgier person. We left promising to keep in touch, which we did.

Some years after we made our first acquaintance I found myself in the position of moving apartments and decided to call on Eric for help. Although I had made use of interior designers before, I quickly discovered that Eric was a different breed, someone whose interest and talent went beyond choosing fabrics and carpeting and the design of window treatments, beyond even reconfiguring the given dimensions of a residence, into something that I can only describe as the inner life of a home. What I mean by this is that he brought his imagination and intuition to the project at hand as much as his acutely informed visual sense and architectural training. He thought big on one's behalf—not by way of lavish trimmings or cunning *objets*, although he's no slouch when it comes to either of these, but by envisioning a space that would meet one's hidden wishes and unspoken dreams. In my case, Eric divined that the writer in me was aching to come out of hiding and declare itself, to which end he helped me feature my endless, beloved collection of books as a main point of the apartment instead of sidelining them.

Gaston Bachelard, the great phenomenologist of houses, writes in his singular book, *The Poetics of Space*, of the "maternal features" of houses, which ideally offer us an image of "protected intimacy." Bachelard insists that "our house is our corner of the world" and that its chief virtue is that it "shelters daydreaming." How we live, in other words, is a reflection of our high-flying fantasies—our wish to sleep in a floating bed of flowers—as well as our concrete realities—our need for more closet space. Eric Cohler shares Bachelard's lyrical view of the extraordinary possibilities available to those of us who look to our corner of the world as more than a place to hang our hats and collect our mail. This book is an introduction to the passion and flair that inform Eric's view of living to our fullest potential in a space that embraces and nurtures us.

—*Daphne Merkin*

PREFACE

As Thomas Wolfe wrote, "You can't go home again." As a young man, intent on my own vision of a well-traveled life, I couldn't have agreed more. Now, as an interior designer at the midpoint of my career, these words ring decidedly untrue. I've learned this lesson the hard way, through trial and error, through exploration and spending time alone as much as among family and friends. I now realize—with what I believe to be some certainty—that I *can* return home, and frequently do. In fact, all of us can take a sense of home with us, each day, in small but meaningful ways.

My first memory of home was an apartment on Chicago's Dearborn Street. With my parents barely out of college and my sister, Jennifer, not yet born, our Irish setter stood guard while I toddled among what today would be labeled midcentury chic furnishings. It was a cozy world of proper respectability juxtaposed with the Danish modern furniture upholstered in vibrant reds and cerulean blues that my parents and their friends revered—or was it merely all that they could afford? Design Research and Marimekko were the Ikea and Jonathan Adler of their day, and their brightly colored fabrics appeared in almost every shelter magazine.

We moved shortly thereafter to Cambridge, Massachusetts, where my father entered graduate school. Home was now a pile of a Second Empire Victorian house filled with antique cast-offs from my grandparents and just the right amount of scattered academic touches to make Dad feel he was a part of the university community. After he graduated and Jennifer was born we packed up again, this time heading for Manhattan, where my father began his psychoanalysis practice on the lower level of an Upper East Side 1880s Italianate brownstone. We lived on the upper three floors and my mother traded in her teak modern and Harvard chairs for English Georgian (most of the unwanted teak somehow, unhappily for me, ending up in my room) juxtaposed with the bold brown and white gestural strokes of Billy Baldwin. Although Baldwin "spoke" only to Mom through magazine layouts and his two books, our house was definitely decorated in "consultation" with this grand master.

The living room was a sea of creams, taupes and beiges with splashes of red. A zebra-skin rug, linen velvet sofas, a Barcelona coffee table—which I have to this day—and George III library chairs and side tables filled the room; a beautiful brown crackle chinoiserie corner cabinet anchored it. The lamps were Qing dynasty and the paintings abstract 1950s American and Italian works. My parents' sitting room and bedroom were completely sheathed in Baldwin's signature brown-and-white Tree of Life print, and the furnishings were a mixture of Directoire and English Regency. Our library was papered in a rich tobacco-colored cork, the woodwork lacquered cream, and the bookshelves mahogany. The upholstery was deep

crimson corduroy and the art and artifacts African tribal pieces. My parents were growing up and so was I. My future view of the world and interiors formed at an early age.

In my designs I take these houses of collective memory, including several others in which I or my family lived, and integrate them into my own studies of interiors and architecture. Among my favorite sources of additional inspiration are the designs of David Adler, Dorothy Draper, Frances Elkins, David Hicks, Jean-Charles Moreux, Karl Friedrich Schinkel, Sir John Soane, and Ludwig Mies van der Rohe. All of these seminal figures had an iconoclastic vision of home that remains relevant, classic, and uncomplicated.

I firmly believe that home, the home to which Thomas Wolfe referred, is eminently portable; fitting on buses, subways, airplanes, cars, and even elevators. Whether climbing Mount Everest with your best friend, driving alone along a deserted highway, or surrounded by thousands of people at a football game, we each carry our own unique vision of home right alongside us, safe and sound.

A family dwelling decorated by Cohler's mother, Jane Supino, in the late 1960s. The penthouse was originally built for Vincent Astor.

CHAPTER I

PASSION

P assion is a fire burning within, propelling us forward. True passions engulf us and quickly become all-consuming. Passion can take many forms: educating yourself exhaustively about one era; researching obscure facts about a piece's provenance; or hunting for a rare item, whether you're a collector pursuing a painting or a designer going to extreme lengths to create a unique fabric.

The French word *frisson* perfectly describes the burning tension passionate people feel. It's an inner electricity that keeps you focused. Tension bridges are held aloft by suspension cables; tensile steel helps buildings stretch skyward; and, similarly, collectors are pulled to acquire objects that elude them. It's an ineffable drive. Once unleashed, passion easily becomes addictive.

Ultimately passion is a quest for beauty, for balance, for harmony. Passion drives us to sate a deep hunger for these seemingly intangible concepts. Possessing a true passion is different than having a mere hobby. Hobbies can be confined to weekends or vacations; passions are full-time loves, like romances. Merely aspiring to acquire what you see that others have—is also not true passion. I call this "the country club syndrome." The classic example is keeping up with the Joneses, whether it's their wallpaper, fabric, sofa, car, or home. Most people want to feel safe, to ensure that they won't be judged for being too outré. They're more comfortable staying within the status quo. False passion often leads people to amass possessions to try and impress others—it stems from insecurity and it's tantamount to demanding acceptance.

If you love something passionately enough, you do whatever it takes to pursue it. In your own home, it's imperative to design spaces that fully support your creative pursuits. After a recent speaking engagement, for example, a woman approached me and said that I had given her the confidence to take books she was storing in her car's trunk—her husband removed them from their library shelves to display golf trophies—and go home and replace them on the shelves. She had sublimated her passion to another person's, an untenable situation. When people don't allow their passions to surface they suffer—and their marriages suffer! Rooms that reflect our passions surround us with our favorite things. They cocoon us. To me, this is ultimate luxury.

A library mantel in Charleston, South Carolina, reveals a juxtaposition of different shapes and objects grouped in odd numbers to create a harmonious arrangement pleasing in symmetry and proportion.

Passion Is Nurtured Within

Style is an attitude, a strong presence, a lack of insecurity. Style doesn't adhere to conventional taste—it transcends taste. Interior designers with style have an innate ability to pull rooms together seamlessly. They develop a vision about the way a space should look, and they make it happen. They don't worry what others think about the space as long as both they and the client are pleased. The majority of people may think that what a truly stylish person has designed is gauche or garish, but it's style nonetheless. The late Diana Vreeland summed it up best when she quipped, "Have good taste, have bad taste, just don't have no taste." What she was saying is to take a stand, to claim a room as your own. Vreeland's own affinity for red lacquer was famously interpreted by Billy Baldwin for her living room—nicknamed the "garden in hell." It was too over the top for many people, but it was recognized as a stylish interior nevertheless. Being true to yourself and creating your own interiors to reflect your style often feels like you're part of an inside joke, one most people won't necessarily understand. Indulging passions, however, is incredibly satisfying and it makes for rooms and homes with true soul.

When a stylish person walks into a restaurant, heads turn. Similarly, when you walk into a room and have a true emotional response to it, you instantly recognize it as fabulous. People who try too hard are never stylish. French women are often cited as inherently knowing how to be stylish, mainly because they know when to stop. It's innate, second nature—it's in the knot of a silk scarf, the angle of a hat, the right amount of jewelry, and, most important, a lack of perceptible artifice.

Style is not simply emulating what you see in a shelter magazine. I know I'm in trouble when a client pulls up a photograph on her iPad and says, "My best friend has this fabric, and she says I should have it, too." Inevitably when I ask why the person likes the fabric the reply is, "Because everyone has it." I do understand how difficult it can be to trust your own instincts. The hardest thing for a designer, I believe, is designing his or her own home. Everyone craves reinforcement, to hear from a third party that the balance of furniture, objects, and color in a room is correct. I have a difficult time designing spaces for myself because I become a hyperperfectionist. I think and rethink everything, which can either be a positive or a negative, depending. To stop, I just have to remind myself that if I were the client, I would fire me for taking too long!

The front porch of a Charleston, South Carolina, single house is painted in a charcoal-gray-and-white checker board design inspired by great Italian piazzas such as the Terrazza Mascagni in Livorno.

Most of us have a fear of not being conventional. Even celebrities with great personal style were known, paradoxically, to be very insecure inside. Marilyn Monroe is a perfect example, as is Greta Garbo. These women became style icons and are admired not merely for the way they looked, but because they were willing to take risks, nurture their own passions, and trust their own instincts.

I have my own style, too, but I have to be sure clients understand that style before recommending an element of it for them. I might suggest painting all the trim in a room or all the doors black, for example. Black trim looks amazing against white grass cloth; the juxtaposition of textures and saturations makes it work. I learned about what black can do for a room by painting the walls in my own living room black as a foil for my black-and-white photography collection, but it took months of experimentation for me to arrive at that result. Before you dismiss a design idea—your own or someone else's—or turn the page in a shelter magazine when your first reaction to a design is that it's just too bizarre, take a second look and try to understand what the unusual element that at first turned you off actually accomplishes or adds to the room. Chances are it will inspire you to try something whimsical or unexpected yourself. Take the risk.

Entrances on several levels provide many opportunities to incorporate welcoming elements into a Charleston house. The exterior, above left, is reminiscent of an Italian loggia. The house's main entry, above right, is flanked by a pair of topiaries with a contemporary shape that contrasts with the classic look of the original nineteenth-century door, lacquered in dove gray. A hall leading to the upper terrace, right, is fitted with a vintage console table, a local find, that holds John Saladino lamps, a Chinese porcelain vase, and Chinese terra cotta figures. The lamb serves as a low-maintenance pet of sorts.

An Italian chandelier anchors a dining room, above, which also
holds monogrammed dining chairs, a Gustavian settee, and a painting
inspired by Fernand Léger. Space beneath a stair, left, is filled
with a table that displays a whimsical collection of disparate objects
whose forms and provenances play off each other unexpectedly.

A sitting room off a guest wing leads to a lushly landscaped garden. The mix of various styles creates a layered look; Biedermeier chairs sit nicely with a contemporary table, a Chinese jar as a centerpiece, and a framed fragment of an Indian mural. Previous pages, left: Light-colored drapes allow plenty of southern sun into a dining room. Previous pages, right: Contemporary cabinetry in the kitchen adds modern convenience to the nineteenth-century structure.

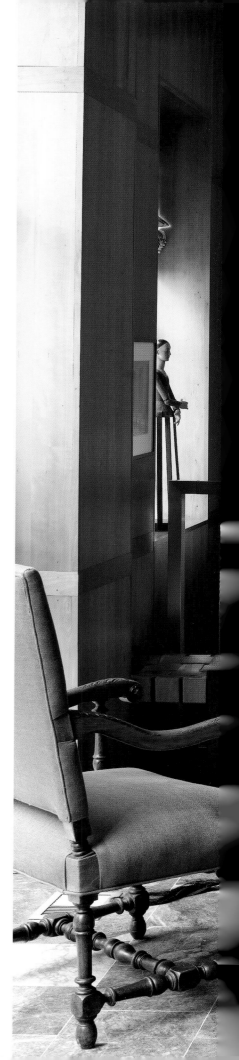

When gathered into the confined space of a mantel, above, a grouping that includes a vintage toy automobile, an Asian sculpture, and a color field painting encourages the eye to linger on the unique attributes of each. Antique French chairs in a sitting area, right, are given an update with brown linen upholstery and are mixed with a contemporary tuxedo sofa, an inherited Mies van der Rohe Barcelona table, and a zebra rug. Upright, clean lines relate to the room's narrow, high-ceilinged architecture.

French doors, above, lead into a master suite. A nineteenth-century French oak table with inescapable personality was a local find. A guest bedroom, opposite, is defined by a rich mixture of antique pieces that suit the house's age and highly graphic fabrics that bring the room into the present.

Comfortable, symmetrically arranged lounge seating is accessorized with fresh blue-and-white pillows in two patterns to create a casual seating area in a garden.

The Power of Passion

It wasn't until I was in law school and doodling plans for how I would like to redesign my lecture halls that I realized I didn't want to be a lawyer. I was twenty-two years old and literally had the epiphany that I hated what I was doing. I realized that everywhere I went I literally studied design, consciously or subconsciously. And so I changed directions. After brief stints in advertising and public relations, I enrolled at Columbia University and wended my way toward design. Now every day is like Christmas. I jump out of bed with alacrity, ready to work on a new project or solve an issue with an existing one. On any given day I may design a new fabric, meet a contractor on a job site, visit an atelier to review trim being applied to curtains, drive out to a quarry with a client to sign off on marble for kitchen counters, or wrap up the day with a speaking engagement at a school or industry event.

When I began my career editors bestowed the moniker "Mixmaster" upon me because I was one of the first of my generation of designers to rethink antiques and use them in a contemporary environment—that's one of my passions. Perhaps you are passionate about golf, travel, or art, but not interior design. A good designer becomes your Virgil and leads you through the various layers of design: color, proportion, form, and historical precedents. If you don't have a designer, work to educate your own eye by reading as much as possible; create an "inspiration" notebook of magazine clippings and visit design showrooms, designer show houses, and period rooms in museums and at National Trust properties.

Anyone designing a room must have real passion—this is nonnegotiable. Without passion you can't assemble an art collection, can't choose fabrics or find the best balance of furniture. The end result will just look flat, unfinished. In a client a designer needs someone that is passionate enough about creating an authentically personal interior that they'll allow the designer to guide them through that process. This is critical for a project's success. Passion is about a clear vision, and even if you don't have a passion for a certain element of interior design at the outset of your project, a good designer will help to instill enthusiasm in you. By the time all is said and done, I bet you will have developed passions of your own.

Marcel Breuer's architecture inspired the glass "living pavilion," right, for which Cohler designed a more vernacular wing. A Dutch door that keeps family pets in while still providing natural ventilation, Provençal shutters, and an axial landscape design inspired by Belgian gardens bring touches of Europe to this Connecticut home.

Mary Wells Lawrence is a good example of a stylish person who knew how to work with a designer to achieve her ends. She was the ne plus ultra of 1960s and 1970s advertising, creating campaigns that literally redefined the industry. She had an acutely honed visual sense for two-dimensional projects, but she hired Billy Baldwin to design her homes in New York and in Cap Ferrat, France. She gave him a clear view of her lifestyle, and he was able to give her a curated home that fit her needs and busy schedule.

Speaking of curating, there is nothing wrong with working within the constraints that objects, family mementos, and art that you truly love place upon your design. My mother has an antique American folk art trade sign shaped like an ax hanging over her desk. I have been known to sneakily take it down and store it

Traditional furnishings converse with contemporary architecture under a narrow stair in a front hall, above. Glass walls and a large skylight dissolve the boundaries between interior and exterior in a dining room that cantilevers over a stream, right.

under her bed when I visit; she immediately hangs it back up when I leave, and this game plays out several times a year. An ax is not what I usually suggest for bedroom décor but she loves it, so there it stays. If I were to be hired to create a room for the Addams family, I would have to work around their totem pole. My point is this: don't sacrifice the things you love just because you feel you should: it's *your* home.

My job as a designer is to create a room and deliver it to the client as a completed project. I always leave room, however, for the later addition of art or books. What many clients don't see is the strategic planning that goes into design. Photograph a room you want to renovate, and literally carry that picture around while you're shopping. Look for pieces that you feel will make your room special and will give it life. Don't try to do everything at once—start with the floor and/or rug and move up from there. Like a building, a room can't stand without a strong foundation. Pick one wall or corner, then think about what challenges it might present. Maybe your room has a structural problem. Say, for example, that you have a dark apartment and you want it to feel more light-filled. Use color and art to direct attention to an interesting object in the room. Add lighting that you can dim down or crank up. Lighting sets mood more than any other single element of design.

I recently finished an apartment on Park Avenue that faced an air shaft, not the famous tree-lined street in front. Apartments that face the interiors of blocks are what I call "courtyard city." But the client still expected her home to fulfill the expectation of luxury suggested by the address. I used full-spectrum bulbs, hidden by a decorative casing, around the perimeters of the windows. They're on a timer so the light is brightest in the morning, when the sun would hit the rooms from the east, then it shifts to correspond to the hours of the day. I added plantation shutters in front of the bulbs and, with the windows and the shutters partially closed, it appears as though sun is shining into the space. Unless the shutters are open, no one notices the trick. Guests just say, "Oh what a beautiful and cozy room." It's full of great art, comfortably scaled furniture . . . and a large television. Televisions are a central part of modern life. Just accept them, and don't try to contrive elaborate ways to hide them. Think of them as performance art pieces—like your own Nam June Paik; at least that way it has presence when it's on. Above all, remember that nothing is proper if you're not passionate about it, if it doesn't make you happy.

To bring light deep into the interior of an apartment on Madison Avenue, right, all walls and ceilings are finished in a high-gloss lacquer. A light fixture with a contemporary design is punched through the ceiling to give the impression of added depth. Modern art and custom shelving filled with a colorful collection of books and *objets*, overleaf, add pops of color to the otherwise predominantly white living room.

Dan Christensen's abstract painting, above, catalyzes an arrangement
of traditional furniture, imbuing a seating area with a contemporary feel.
In the daytime, right, a living room's many reflective or highly polished
surfaces bounce sunlight throughout the space.

Gleaming surfaces that keep a low-ceilinged kitchen, above, feeling open and airy include transparent bar stools and polished limestone flooring tiles; the custom banquette's Lucite feet continue the theme. The forms in a Donald Baechler print also relate subtly to the pattern on the shade's fabric. A custom crystal chandelier, left, crowns a dining room that gets its verve from a play of dark and light tones; the drapery and area rug are from the designer's collection for Lee Jofa, and the English limestone mantel is designed by Cohler as well.

Vaulting the ceiling of an otherwise narrow hallway, above, gives it a sense of breadth and height; a runner in the same color family as the nursery's wall-to-wall carpeting helps lead the eye into the larger space. Dark tones injected into a den, opposite, give it a coziness; modern touches of stainless steel on the light fixture and coffee table, and Lucite on the desk, keep it contemporary.

Ice-blue tones lend a relaxed glamour to a master bedroom suite, above. The color's appearance on fabrics—layered curtains, settee upholstery, headboard, and bedding —helps the room feel warm despite the cool palette. In a nod to tradition, a mirrored dressing table and stool, left, create a vignette reminiscent of 1930s glamour.

CHAPTER 2

MAKING YOUR OWN GRAND TOUR

Traditionally the scions of great English and, later, American families were sent on an extended trip to Europe, quaintly referred to as "the Continent." This grand tour was not only to give them first-hand experience of European art, architecture, and history, but to help inform their tastes and to give them the opportunity to bring back furniture, decorative accessories, paintings and sculptures—things that spoke to them but also spoke of the past. These objects showed people back home that the owner was erudite, that he or she had—with help or not—begun to amass valuable antiquities. Such collections made one appear learned and established.

It's really no different today in many ways. Whether we walk downtown or venture to Asia, we want to bring something back with us. Our way of seeing is inevitably informed by the things and places we encounter, and we bring that new sensibility home. Sometimes it translates into how you shape your environment: even traveling around your own block can yield inspiration if you're open to it. Say you're walking down the street and you notice a tree branch moving in the wind that is creating an unusual or striking shadow on the pavement. Suddenly you think, "That's a great design! Maybe I should paint a silhouette of a large branch with leaves on it on my bedroom wall."

Items you select from your travels add dimension to your home. In a sense you're hunting for trophies, just like people who went on safari in the late nineteenth or early twentieth centuries. They would travel to Africa and bring back their finds as mounted lion heads or zebra rugs. People today, many of whom have taken advantage of modern business opportunities to make money in a hurry, either don't necessarily have

**Ornately carved legs on a console table designed by Gerald Bland
makes it a perfect, if counterintuitive, match for the James Brooks painting
above; the sinuosity of both pieces makes them a sympathetic pair.**

a liberal arts education or a passion for collecting, but would like to learn more about the arts—if only they could find the time. They may be educated in technology or they may be excellent at raising venture capital, but they may not have been fortunate to have had the experience of falling in love with a painting.

That's where a designer can help. We become teachers and curators at once. I always make a point of educating my clients by taking them to museums, galleries, and shops. I also want people to read as much as possible about what they're about to invest in and to understand the background of a piece before making a purchase. I always recommend research before acquisition. Sometimes the reason people want to collect, even if they don't have a passion for it, is purely out of conspicuous consumption. They want to have friends over and hear them say, "Wow, that's a real Warhol!" But in my experience, people are far more impressed by carefully curated groupings of quirky or unusual objects—hand-painted snuffboxes, say.

So when I go out with clients as a hunter looking for exotic prey, it forms a grand tour type of experience, even if we don't leave town. It's up to me to be the guide, to be like Virgil in Dante's *Divine Comedy*: I map out the journey clients will take with me, but make sure to let them learn some lessons of their own along the way. The important thing to remember about educating your eye is to expose yourself to a larger world, preferably one more cosmopolitan than where you live. Kitschy-but-offbeat souvenirs, works by local artists, or furniture that's got an interesting shape but has seen better days—not just expensive art or antiques—can all become trophies. They will be something you're proud of, something with a story, something you found yourself instead of just opening a catalog or buying off the rack.

You might wonder: why bother in the age of the Internet, when you can see so much online? Simply because it is completely different to see an object in three dimensions. Every single time, without exception, when I've make a purchase online, I've been disappointed. Either the scale is wrong, the fabric doesn't feel the way I thought it would, there are condition issues, or the level of craftsmanship is poor. I usually end up sending a piece back or giving it away, making online shopping an expensive and time-consuming process. So I have learned the hard way to revert to do what I was originally trained to do—actually sit in a chair, look at it from every angle, get down underneath it with a flashlight and see how it was constructed. You just can never rely on someone else's description of an item.

A vignette of art and accessories from various eras and provenances gives an Upper East Side condominium living room a decidedly international flair.

Take a Grand Tour
No Matter What the Itinerary

There's a wonderful painting by Caspar David Friedrich, *Wanderer Above the Sea of Fog*, of a young man standing on the top of a mountain and contemplating the mist below and beautiful snow-capped peaks in the distance. He's completely absorbed with the beauty of what he sees. It's one of my favorite pieces of art of all time, and I would love to design a room inspired by it someday. Think about what inspires you: if it's pop culture, then rewatch your favorite movie, stream your favorite music video. If you love animals, go to the zoo and look at seals playing in the water; if you love the beach, drive out to the nearest pier and sit on it for half an hour. Take a few minutes to analyze what it is about the visual atmosphere of your favorite type of "scene." Is it the colors, the furniture, the fashion? Is it the characteristic design of the era? A great place to begin designing is by literally compiling lists of your favorite things, moods, colors—you probably acknowledge them all the time, but in a vague or subconscious way. One of the tasks interior designers are able to do, by training, is to make client preferences concrete, but you can do it too, by just stopping to think about what elements of your favorite things intrigue you or make you happy.

Caspar David Friedrich's *Wanderer Above the Sea of Fog*, left, reveals the goals for any grand tour, whether around the world or around town—wonder, discovery, and contemplation. A collection of English, Swedish, and Chinese ceramics and a photograph of Brasília by French native Elliott Erwitt, right, bring reminders of past travels home to a West Coast dining room. Overleaf: A curated selection of objects from around the globe continues the grand tour theme in a living room. A T. H. Robsjohn-Gibbings klismos chaise and a Jean-Michel Frank coffee table anchor the collection.

My firm sometimes takes clients to Europe, when we need to acquire a lot of pieces for a large project or the clients have a particular sensibility for antiques. We'll go through the flea markets in London and Paris or visit the Milan furniture fair. The best part of this, besides the opportunity of getting to know them well, is that they are focused on the task at hand instead of being constantly interrupted on cell phones or email like when they're at home. They can make informed, considered purchases. Try to give yourself that quiet space as well when you're looking for new objects.

I recently took a client to Paris, where we found incredible midcentury modern bar stools. They were brass and they had a unique shape—I had never seen anything like them. But there were only two of them. What to do if you find yourself in this situation, either with objects you find abroad or at your local flea market or a nearby estate sale? Remember that you can commission a local artisan to make more. We had four more stools made in Long Island City, New York. Problem solved, and the owners are happy to know they have a set unlike anybody else's.

We also bought a wonderful Jean-Michel Frank sofa. Its 1940s lines were perfectly proportioned. We found paintings, too, beautiful abstracts. The point being not only that the client was delighted with the quantity of items—they liked the objects themselves well enough—but when they arrived back in the U.S. the excitement was prolonged, because they had gone somewhere interesting to find them, brought them home, and they were going to have something that their friends didn't have, something that they were passionate about. It's easier to open a catalog or a new web browser, but the payoff for taking a side trip out of your way or following up a listing in your local paper is much better. A shopping excursion can qualify as an adventure even if it's just to a street in your own hometown you've never been down before.

Where to Look

I generally have favorite cities and favorite vendors, and after you begin trolling for treasure on a regular basis, you will have yours too. In the U.S. I love to shop in West Palm Beach on South Dixie Highway, because I like the fact that it tends to be a mix of pieces from different estates. Some people feel they're junk shops—I don't. The shop owners buy from many estates that were last decorated in the 1950s and 1960s; the heirs don't want to spend the money to send things up to up to New York for auction, so they sell them to these galleries. We're not talking the highest quality that exists, but we are talking about period pieces you can't easily find today. If you value pieces for their personality more than for their actual value, these types of design areas are for you. Say you find an iconic Pace dining table built in chrome and brass . . . couple it with chairs you inherited from your grandparents and voilà: layering.

Mixes of high- and low-priced pieces help stretch any decorating budget; the window treatments in a living room, above, come from the Shade Store, and mix well with antique pieces. A dining area, left, embraces the casual Californian indoor/outdoor lifestyle; one bright vase is all the embellishment the verdant landscaping needs.

I also shop Los Angeles's La Cienega and La Brea Boulevards. Stores there are great because you can usually look at their inventory online, then take a trip to see an item in person and kick the tires, so to speak. And the best part is that there will be other things there you didn't see on the website that will tempt you: that will be part of the art of discovery. Try going into the basement or upstairs, don't just stay on the main floor. Back rooms are usually where owners keep things they don't think will sell right away—it's where I find the best things of all. Rummage. Gallery dealers especially encourage you to root around. I found some absolutely gorgeous midcentury abstract paintings at the Spanierman Gallery warehouse in New York. Don't be afraid to ask dealers to let you have a look around—it takes doing it a few times to get over being intimidated to ask, but it's almost always worth it. And it makes a better story.

Look for special items—the jewels to adorn the setting that is your basic, boxy room. Resist the temptation to buy something if you don't feel a true desire for it. Save your money for the pieces that truly speak to you—don't grab things just because you think you need to fill up shelves. Look for pieces that could anchor a room. The great thing about decorating your home is that it's not necessarily about shopping—it's about building a nest for yourself that will remind you of adventures and good times you've had. Pieces with funny, awkward, or even just long stories behind them make home feel more like home. Have a relationship with everything in it. Get out of your comfort zone, whatever it is—whether it's ordering from catalogs, going to the same three stores all the time, or never leaving the state—and put yourself into a different environment.

Photograph the room you're looking to fill, both actually and metaphorically—carry around a shot of your room in your wallet while you're shopping. Look for pieces that will animate the space. If it's a white rental box, you can still turn it into an expression of yourself and make the generic special by introducing a few key pieces. Think of them as "conversation pieces" if that helps. Would you have anything to tell a guest about the object you're thinking of buying? Is there something about the way it's carved or the material that intrigues you? If not, leave it in the shop. Just as you try not to invite guests to a dinner party who are drab and boring, don't invite in pieces that don't have personality, either.

Take your own grand tour by jumping in the car and hitting a garage sale, by riding a bike to look at a building in your town you know is architecturally significant but that you've never really stopped to look at or photograph, or by plane to a location you've never been. Inspiration is everywhere.

Chocolate lacquer wallpaper adds dimension to a coffered ceiling, above right; the treatment is a simpler take on elaborate European precedents. Honey-toned cabinetry and flooring, right, warm up a kitchen; a David Weeks light fixture adds whimsy.

Black-and-white photography in alternating black and white frames adds
structure and interest to a stairwell, above and above right, giving the space the
aura of a gallery. A large-format photograph by Matthew Pillsbury presides over
a library, right, where Holly Hunt furniture mingles with antique artifacts from
Africa and Asia. Overleaf: A black accent wall and a steel bench covered in gray
Mongolian lamb add masculine details to a master bedroom. Side tables and
accompanying lamps are mixed, rather than matched, for interest.

Texture reigns in this guest bedroom. The hallway leading to it, left, is lined in grass cloth to set the stage for other earth tones that follow. A wooden, barrel-backed wing chair and a throw blanket with curly fibers, above, continue the theme. Previous pages: A graciously sized sitting area in a master bedroom suite is carpeted with a luxurious, wall-to-wall, silk-wool rug to keep bare feet cozy. Over-leaf: A top-floor workspace's painted gables help the room feel finished; grass cloth wallpaper and custom built-in storage add sophistication; skylights, braced by earthquake rods, flood the area with natural light to encourage productivity.

Heavily textured grass cloth wallpaper, above and above
right, indicates a transition from light-filled upper levels to
the darkened media room in the basement, below right.

Let Your Imagination Take You Places

When you go to see a preview exhibition at an auction house, the grand tour essentially comes to you. There will always be a definite point of view, which is very important. The collection has been culled and pieces selected by, perhaps, the English furniture department at Christie's. It's valuable to go and see "the best" of what the most highly trained specialists have been able to bring to market. These might be things that you wouldn't necessarily have seen before, or things that haven't been on the market since the original owner purchased them thirty to forty years ago. Auction houses arrange objects in a way that makes it easy for clients to see and understand the connection between them or what era they belong to. Auction houses also give you a guarantee that a piece is authentic—if you can prove it isn't, they'll take it back. I once bought a piece of folk art that turned out not to be by the artist they said it was. It had been repainted on an old canvas in such a skillful manner they couldn't detect the forgery until we got a second opinion. But that happens very rarely.

A snapshot of a zebra taken on safari, left, directly inspired a fabric with a repeat that stretches the full length of the animal's body, right. The footstool sits in front of a trompe l'œil dado panel inspired by Jean-Michel Frank and Christian Béard's design for the Institut Guerlain in Paris, and is set off by floor-length curtains of a related chocolate hue detailed with a rickrack trim.

If you happen to live in or be in New York City, try to go to a Christie's home sale. They do one every other month. They feature pieces designers have taken from their warehouses for deaccession, and they set everything up in cozy little vignettes. This is a good way to learn about the value of certain pieces, and you can get great ideas for how to arrange things in a room as well. You can also often get incredible large-scale art from the 1960s and 1970s that will anchor a room. The estimates are usually extremely low because the artists are considered passé by "the industry" but, first, that doesn't mean they're going to be passé tomorrow, and, second, if you love the colors, and love what the painting says to you, grab it. Since so many houses and apartments are built without fireplaces now, large art serves as a fantastic focal point. All you need is a little imagination to take a piece that may seem unusual at first and make it work for you.

If you can't travel, look at past scrapbooks or travel photos to inspire you. That process helped me create a fabric collection for Lee Jofa. I put my favorite paintings and images into a folder—works by Rothko, my favorite city, Stockholm, images of Balenciaga dresses because I like the draping. I put in patterns from nature, like waves crashing on the shore. If you can't create your own—although it's getting easier to find services that will either enlarge photos for you to poster-size or to print an image on fabric— search for fabrics in colors or patterns that remind you of a place or a view you love. Even if your guests don't make the connection, you will, and having a room designed by you, for you, will make it all the more comfortable. I followed a similar process with my lighting collection for Visual Comfort: I started sketching designs based on a coat rack from the 1930s, and developed the shape into a sconce. Don't be afraid to think about getting pieces custom made—chances are there's a local artisan near you who can help you and probably for less than you think. I guarantee that they will love to stretch their talents by working on a creative commission.

Cohler at Machu Picchu, left, a place that deepened his appreciation for the sophistication of early Inca civilization and that influenced him to create a collection of trim based on patterns passed on to him by its descendants. A view that unfolds to reveal an Upper East Side living room gradually, right, was also inspired by the narrow site of the pre-Colombian city.

Art and accessories can bring international flavor to any space. A Henry Moore sculpture, above, reclines on a coffee table while Turkish ikat pillows add a pop of indigo to a sofa and a contemporary take on a traditional nineteenth-century portrait watches over the room. Even a small, marble-topped, French Empire table, right, contributes to the room's carefully curated theme by holding a Matisse print, a Christopher Spitzmiller lamp, a fragment of a bust, and a decorative bowl thrown by a Long Island artisan. Previous pages: Furniture from a mix of periods imbues a contemporary apartment with a rich sense of history. A coffee table in the style of John Dickinson and an Alberto Giacometti Tête de Femme floor lamp anchor a seating area defined by a pair of Louis XVI bergères, a Gustavian side chair that dates to the 1780s, and a Late Regency, William IV–era sofa.

When Cohler moved floors in the same building, he used it as an opportunity to rethink the arrangement of artwork he had grown accustomed to in the first space and to experiment with color, texture, and pattern. A Charles Lutz limited-edition Brillo Box, above, serves as a side table that holds a round English match striker and a museum reproduction of an Indian sculpture from the ninth century. Cohler found that wenge-wood walls polished to an eggshell finish, above right, helped to accent the sinuous forms of the furniture, particularly a late-eighteenth-century Irish stool covered in yellow kid leather. The walls also serve to outline the head of a fifteenth-century Chinese Buddha, below right, and to make the vibrant colors of a Warhol flower print and a contemporary painting with a solid yellow background pop.

Wasabi green energizes the walls and ceiling in a dining room, left, and animates its art and furniture, including an English grandfather clock with a dark green lacquer finish and *Woman with White Mask*, a 1998 photograph by Michael Thompson. Overleaf: In opposite corners of the dining room, above left and far right, an English linen press stands in as a breakfront while the round form of a yellow Dale Chihuly basket is set off by a black-and-white marble-topped console table and an iconic Marilyn print by Andy Warhol. Carefully chosen art—a drawing by Frank Gehry and a fashion photo—imbue a wet bar with elegance.

Gloss paint in a rich color, above, on a study's ceiling—every room's "fifth wall"—adds personality to an otherwise straightforward space. Edwardian reading chairs covered in gray and white linens and a nineteenth-century Qing Dynasty cabinet repurposed as a bookcase support the room's function. Somber walls imbue a dining room, left, with a formal, traditional feeling, although the selection of furniture remains unchanged from its other incarnation in a wasabi-green dining room.

Wrapping the walls and ceiling in one continuous color gives a home office, above, a unique identity within the apartment. A late Georgian architect's desk and Biedermeier-style stool add a sense of history. Strong lines help an eighteenth-century English library chair, right—upholstered in linen and detailed with brown and beige ribbons—harmonize with floor-to-ceiling Venetian blinds installed to ameliorate awkward visual lines created by window frames of different sizes and shapes. A nineteenth-century Venetian baroque settee and an antique side chair introduce curves. Previous pages: Vignettes recomposed after Cohler moved from one floor to another within the same building.

Primarily functional spaces, such as hallways and kitchens, are often overlooked but can provide unique opportunities for introducing character. An early-eighteenth-century equestrian portrait, above, draws the eye to a similarly shaped figurine farther down the hall. A late Roman torso, above and below right, invites guests to a stairwell featuring art by Jenny Holzer and Charles Lutz. A faux deer trophy mounted in an unexpected location, above right, adds dimension to a galley-style kitchen.

USE WHAT IS DOMINANT
IN A CULTURE
TO CHANGE IT QUICKLY

Inspiration Comes from Unlikely Sources

Edith Wharton is a great example of someone who pursued a passion at all costs. She was so passionate about writing, in fact, that she sacrificed her marriage for it. I find that inspiring—so inspiring that I designed a room based on her library. I also find the Pantheon in Rome majestic, so I used it as inspiration for a shower Kohler asked me to design for them for their main showroom in Wisconsin. The Pantheon was first used as a Roman temple, then a Catholic church, and it has a famous open oculus at the top, so if it rains, the rain comes right in. I found its relationship with water, the elements, baptism—and all its incarnations—very striking. This led me to think of it in relationship to a bath and the mini rebirth bathing gives us every day, and hence to the shower. When Jeanne-Claude and Christo's *The Gates* was installed in Central Park in 2005, it inspired me to use billowy fabric panels instead of more-expected doors on a bathroom cupboard. Inspiring people, buildings, and art can help to guide you in big ways, like the design of an entire room, or in small ways, such as on decorative details. All add meaning to your space.

If you love and are inspired by a certain era, look up books published in that period. Say you love the 1950s, for example. Any room you find in a design book from that decade will have a completely different palette from colors that are available in the stores today—tastes evolve. But you can replicate period colors by

The Gates installation by Jeanne-Claude and Christo, left, inspired a solution to a design problem in a powder room, right. Thick fabric panels in lieu of doors screen the storage space.

custom-mixing them if you can't find them on a standard paint chip. Technology helps us today; most paint stores have a widget that can scan any color and tell the clerk the perfect mix of dyes to use to achieve it. Or turn your mother's favorite dress from the 1940s into an entire room if you like: use the fabric's color for the walls, the way it drapes to guide you on which fabrics to use for the window treatments, and the pattern to help you find similar trims or accent pillows. Once you identify something that inspires you, like a painting, a photograph, even an impression, explode its components exponentially. It can be anything you've found on your own grand tour—physical or mental—a strange old wooden doll at a flea market, your favorite photograph from your last vacation, or a piece of art you love but could never actually afford to own. Any room that contains meaningful references for you will satisfy you more than an impersonal room filled with things you aren't passionate about or feel that you "should" own but don't actually use or love.

Edith Wharton's library at The Mount, above, inspired a space in the 1999 Kips Bay Decorator Show House, right. It redefines preconceived notions about what a library should be by replacing the contemplative desk with a luxurious bathtub. Previous pages: Concentric patterns created by the Pantheon's deeply coffered ceiling inspired Cohler to create a gray-and-white striped luxury shower for the Kohler showroom in Wisconsin; a light monitor takes the place of the original structure's oculus and floods the space with radiance.

In a guest bedroom suite, above and right, dogs from Cohler's youth live on in the Unleashed fabric he created for Lee Jofa. Sisal wall-to-wall carpeting and a Slim Aarons print, *Nice Pool*, showing C.Z. Guest and her son, hint at the beachside location.

A soft palette unites decorative objects from various eras in an Upper East Side apartment. A sculpture by Gérard Le Roux, left, relates to the pastel hues of paintings featuring classical subject matter and a Chinese ginger jar, left and above, while a rug with a circular motif brings the traditional furniture into the twenty-first century.

In lieu of a wall, a Barcelona daybed, above, separates one large room into distinct living and dining spaces. George Waite's painting, left, adds a vibrant hit of intense color to an apartment serenly focused on neutral hues. Previous pages: The steel arms and white leather upholstery of Knoll dining chairs echo the curved lines and color of a Victor Matthews painting that sets the mood. Lacquered wallcovering by Phillip Jeffries adds to the brilliant-white theme.

A narrow butler's pantry gets an uplifting detail in the form of boldly patterned David Hicks wallpaper on the ceiling, above; great houses of eras past often emphasized the ceiling with decoration. In a modern twist on the traditional pairing of oil painting and chair, right, the historical precedent is updated with a contemporary piece of art and a fresh interpretation of a classic campaign stool.

CHAPTER III

CURATE YOUR SPACE

Certain people are born with a passion for collecting. Continually hunting for the next example to fit into their collection fulfills an innate need. It's not simply hoarding, but the *want* to acquire something wonderful. Art collectors are the classic example: they may have hundreds of pieces of art, but they can always find room for one more. People collect wine, couture clothing, cars, and, as relates to interior design, pieces of furniture and decorative objects. If you want to start collecting, you must make a commitment to educate yourself, and you have to develop a passion for whatever it is that you start to collect.

A collector is someone who is never content to stop acquiring. I've met collectors who have ten fantastic paintings on their walls but twenty more under the bed. Some have literally thousands of pieces of porcelain. They may not even be on display—they may be tucked away in cabinets or closets because their house doesn't have enough display space. Sometimes a collection is based on a quirky subject. One client collected clown dolls, and even had us design clown crown molding for her family room. They can't quit. If they see a great piece somewhere that fits into their collection, they simply have to purchase it—and if they can't afford it, they'll figure out how to get the money. It's an addiction. I've even heard an anecdote about someone who stole art, not so he could resell it, but just to hang in his home and pile it up against the walls.

I'm guilty of being an obsessive collector, so I understand this impulse. I understand that you can have a relationship with a painting even though it's an inanimate object. You fall in love, you fall out of love, you decide you want to put it up on a shelf for awhile, you know you'll bring it down and look at it sometimes, but you would never, ever part with it. It's like an old friend you call up after many years and have lunch with, or the former lover you've never quite stopped being attracted to.

An air of luxury permeates a stairwell reinterpreted as a gallery where photographs are hung salon-style. A railing wrapped in Hermès leather begins a dark-brown accent color scheme continued by a David Hicks custom runner and subtly patterned linen wallcovering.

I own art that I would never sell in my lifetime. I would rather have this art around me in an apartment than light or a view. I have four studies for paintings Edward Hopper drew in the 1950s: a car, hotel room, a deer, and a woman on a sofa. I also have a John Singer Sargent, a small drawing of a building in Venice from his sketchbooks from the early 1900s. I also couldn't sell most of my photography collection—Abbotts, Arbus, Sherman, Steichen, Stieglitz.

That's not to say that all collectors automatically become inseparable from every piece they purchase; the key is to keep collecting. Some of my art I thought I loved when I bought it, but later decided I could let go. Something else came along and caught my fancy, and I traded up, or I sold one piece to finance another. I had a Mark Rothko oil study on paper; unfortunately as the economy began to fray, I had to sell it. I sold it for exactly what I paid. I didn't make money, but still I got my money's worth because I enjoyed it while I owned it. I first purchased the Rothko because I had always wanted to own a work by him, so I bought the best I could afford. I'm glad I stretched to make it happen and had the privilege of having it in my home for several years.

Clients occasionally see a piece of mine and say, "I have to have that." Sometimes I'll give it to them for what I paid for it—the goal of collecting for me isn't to invest or make money, it's purely for visceral pleasure. If I can see the client is passionate about a piece and gets truly excited, it's like a meeting of kindred spirits. Truthfully, I could probably be convinced to part with most of the 600 works I own, except for 50 or so core pieces. Of course, then I would run out and start building up my collection all over again.

One example of something does not make a collection; to me a collection is a minimum of at least half a dozen like pieces. One piece of art is a pleasant focal point to hang over a sofa, but it's not a collection. A true collection helps to draw your eye around a room. I help clients hang or position art in a concerted way, the way a curator would in a museum. Together, we curate what they own and create a definite focus. A big, random collage of work can detract from an overall effect of clarity. We try to hang art and photography in a linear or vertical fashion or group items with a similar sensibility or color palette, even if they're from different eras. This helps you actually see the art and not just a mass of images.

Organizing art in a rational or technically perfect way is difficult, even for the pros. I'm guilty myself: my own photography collection became so large I had to hang it floor to ceiling in my stairwell. It's not ideal, but it's what works for me and, practically speaking, it fills up what can be empty, awkward space in a lively way. Don't underestimate the use of collections to draw attention away from your house's imperfections, either. I have to feel good in my space. I don't want to live in a white box. Sometimes I fantasize that my perfect apartment would contain just one or two great paintings on the scale of a Rothko—but I know in my heart that's not going to happen. Take practical considerations into account when building a collection and remember that quirky and personal is preferable to over the top or forced.

To hang a collection of art or arrange a grouping of decorative objects, I generally take the largest piece first and gradually spread ancillary pieces around it. Think about it as if you're designing a house: start by planning the largest, main space then let the other spaces serve that. Group smallish pieces together if possible, at eye level, to keep them from getting "lost" on a wall or shelf. For one client who wanted to be able to display an enormous collection all at once, I created a gallery based on an idea I first saw in the Soane Museum in London. In the nineteenth century, Sir John Soane created a system of hinged panels, joined along one side, for holding art. Each "leaf" holds several pieces. Philip Johnson also employed a similar system in his private museum on his Connecticut grounds. In a revised interpretation, my firm often hangs art on modular bars so you can shift the art around whenever you feel like it. In this way, art doesn't become static wallpaper that you stop truly seeing. Collectors love to be able to rearrange, mix and match—it becomes another way for them to see and reinterpret their collection.

Collectors never stop acquiring, so the way their collections are displayed shouldn't stop evolving, either. Think about a place you've lived that had a great view—even if it was Central Park or the ocean, at some point, you probably stopped focusing on it every day. In the same way, a painting or object that never moves eventually blends or melds into the background. When you live with anything day in and day out, you can't help but take it for granted. Like your partner, you have to make an effort to romance a room, too. Rearrange things at least once a year. Whether they're grand or humble, you'll appreciate them all over again.

We All Use Our Past to Define Our Here and Now

People often turn to the past for examples of good taste. It's vetted. Safe. That's also why so many people reinvent their personal pasts—so that they seem more established. Celebrities do it all the time. People move to New York from a small town and then all of a sudden they claim to have been raised in a very different way than they really were. They may say they grew up in Kentucky on a bucolic horse farm. In reality their father may have been a groom or a veterinarian. People love to reinvent their past to serve a certain purpose. It's the same with interior design—people simply feel more confident building on the foundation of things that are considered timeless. It's easier.

My education in interior design started as a child. My family founded a clothing company in 1870 that later became part of Hart Schaffner Marx—at one point the largest men's clothing manufacturer in America. The company's success allowed them to build important houses on Chicago's North Shore. My great-grandmother visited the Century of Progress International Exposition, the Chicago World's Fair of 1933, saw architect George Fred Keck's "House of Tomorrow" there, and called him. She told him she'd like a new house. And he said, "Fantastic, I'll build you the House of Tomorrow." Her reply was, "No, listen carefully, that's not what I want. What I want is the house of the day *after* tomorrow." This was in the middle of the Great Depression, but she had it built in Lake Forest anyway. She tore down the house her father had built in the 1880s—a large pile of a Queen Anne monstrosity on the shores of Lake Michigan—and she replaced it in 1937 with the first true Bauhaus residence in Chicago.

My grandmother, Betty, was a chic woman with her own sense of style. She was tall, blonde, and willowy, rail thin—a model's body that dressmakers adored, but her face was not that of a conventional beauty by any means. Once she put her makeup on and was dressed, though, all eyes were on her. When she walked into a room, people would turn and look at her stylish clothes. She was like Wallis Simpson and Diana Vreeland—she knew how to pull herself together. The French term *jolie laide* definitely applied. She would spend two hours putting her face on. As a child it was kind of frightening to me, but at the time, women wore heavier makeup.

She had innate style and she adored fashion—the family's love of clothing was definitely in her blood. She had an encyclopedic knowledge of fashion designers, and not a day went by when she didn't read *Women's Wear Daily*. She wore Balenciaga, Valentino, and Missoni long before they were popular here. She would go

A study by J. C. Leyendecker for an advertisement for Kuppenheimer, a menswear clothing line established by Cohler's family, and which also held the contract for the U.S. Navy and Army officers' uniforms during World War II and into the 1920s.

to Paris almost every year to the couture shows. In fact, she had gone to Europe every season since she was a little girl. The only time she didn't go was during World War II.

In 1968, my grandparents built a Bauhaus-style house in Palm Springs. They recreated or reinterpreted the house her parents had built in Lake Forest, but on a golf course. It had the characteristic Bauhaus features: the extensive use of glass, a flat roof, a rational floor plan, and interior courtyards. But it was more layered than the Bauhaus, an interesting combination we referred to in the family as "the Bauhaus meets the baroque." This was influenced by what Edward Durell Stone was doing at the time. He began as a strict modernist, but later began to adapt elements of classical architecture into his work. My grandmother was very influenced by that. She had the house decorated by someone who had worked for Ted Garber, so it was very much in the mode of Billy Haines. All the furniture was custom made for the house.

She had a dressing room the size of most people's bedrooms annexed to her master suite and everything was arranged by color. I remember that clearly. She also always had fresh flowers everywhere. The house had an enormous sunken living room with a Picasso over the fireplace, that was the ne plus ultra that helped fuel my love of art.

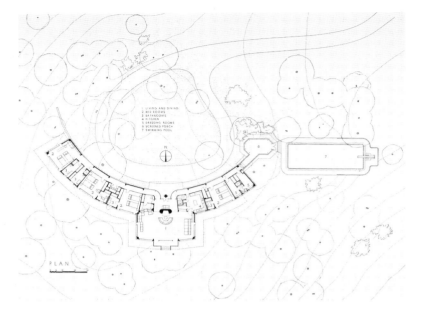

The floor plan, left, and exterior, right, of the Bauhaus-inspired home Cohler's great-grandmother commissioned Keck & Keck to build in Chicago in the 1930s. It was one of the first structures built in the style in the Midwest. The living room, below right, featured retractable glass walls and all the furnishings and fittings—down to the ashtrays—were built-in.

My mother, who married into that side of the family, was also a huge influence. She trained as an artist and could copy a Braque or a Picasso with precision. When my grandparents bought my parents a brownstone on the Upper East Side, my mother proceeded to decorate it with the help of "Billy Baldwin." As far as I know she never met him . . . but she had his book and she turned her talent for emulating designs to creating a home for her growing family. She found his brown-and-white toile fabric and she covered the entire master bedroom in it—she upholstered the walls with it, covered the sofa with it, and made a bedspread and curtains out of it. She installed white bookcases and blue-and-white Delft tiles around the fireplace. I loved the color combination, and I still use chocolate and blue in my work to this day.

She also decorated our country house in East Hampton, near Georgica Pond. We found an 1899 carriage house built by McKim, Mead & White, and moved it from its original site to four acres surrounded by meadow. Julian Neski, a modernist architect who was hot in the 1970s, renovated it. My mother's interiors were quite clean and clear, distilled down to the essence of what I think a Hamptons house should be. In front of the fireplace there were white bouclé sofas—large, comfortable models stuffed with down—and a beautiful coffee table made out of cast iron shaped like bamboo. Everything sat on a large fox rug that anchored the room. The huge space was perfectly symmetrical, with French doors on one side of the room, and on the other, bookcases as well as my father's antique half-hull sailing models.

One of our terraces ended up being painted by Andy Warhol. My parents rented the house to Halston one summer, who was friendly with Andy, and they had a couple of wild parties where somehow cans of paint came out. Their legacy to us—which my parents didn't actually appreciate at the time—was this brightly

painted brick terrace. It was the last time my parents ever let strangers stay in the house. It was probably one of the most beautiful houses I've ever seen. Even to this day I stand by that statement.

My parents' marriage dissolved, and when my mother remarried she actually hired a decorator for the first time. She first wanted to hire a well-known alumna who had recently left Parish-Hadley, but when she quoted a price of $200,000 for the living room alone, my mother and stepfather decided to find a young designer to work with, instead. She hired David Lawrence. They decorated two rooms a year. Working together for three years, they did a terrific job.

This is where I come in. I was a freshman in college and I kept piping up, mouthing off, giving my opinions whether solicited or not, but my mother thought some of the ideas were pretty good. So she asked me to help redesign the bedroom. It was the first room I had published—in a small magazine that's now defunct, but it was a start. It was serendipitous that it ran, but at the time I had no intention of becoming a designer; I was headed to law school.

We all mine our past to find our future. Without past references I personally can't move forward. I need to be inspired by the past as prologue. Many designers think only of what the future should look like, and create very contemporary rooms and pieces. That is not what I do best—my forte is creating curated, elegant-but-comfortable, lived-in-looking rooms. My foundation is classical training, mixed with personal experience of some spaces that were fairly radical for their time.

My talent is balancing the past, the present, and, to some degree, the future. I travel easily between different eras. I can reach back to the sixteenth century or fast-forward to 2012 with a stop along the way in 1950. I've designed rooms around eighteenth-century Old Master paintings as well as huge Chihuly glass sculptures. I've also woven in colors drawn directly from the marble in fifteenth-century Venetian Gothic palazzi—a very soft, muted, oatmeal stone I can't find anywhere else. Replicating that is the kind of challenge I thrive on. In a landmarked 1930s house built by Edward Durell Stone, I renovated its outdated kitchen with my own touches about how I imagined the era; I added walnut cabinets, silver-plated hardware, Danby marble counters, trough lighting, skylights, and black-and-white linoleum floors. It feels like an authentic continuation. There's no question that my past has taught me to look at the bones of architecture and art, and informs my present in a meaningful way. Yours can, too.

The A. Conger Goodyear House, above right, designed by Edward Durell Stone in 1938. It was left uninhabited after Goodyear's death in 1964 and was saved from demolition in 2005 by the World Monuments Fund. It reminds Cohler strongly of his great-grandmother's house, so he bought it and spent four years restoring it. Cohler's poodles, Olivia and Griffin, right, frolic in the courtyard in front of a mural original to the house.

A complete renovation of the Goodyear House kitchen, above, added modern amenities, such as a breakfast bar, while restoring period details, such as the windows and doors and checkerboard linoleum floor. Cohler placed sculptures throughout the property, right, which had previously contained many. Outdoor armchairs and ottomans provide casual seating between the backyard's swimming pool and reflecting pool, opposite.

Art Fuels the Soul

For me art and books are needs, like oxygen and water. Wherever I live or work, it's critical that there is art around me. It takes an enormous amount of energy for an artist to create a painting, and the canvas harnesses that energy. In turn, I channel that energy. Looking at Renaissance paintings energizes me particularly; next time you go to a museum take a moment to think about what an artist is trying to say through color, form, structure, and texture. When you're having a bad day, take thirty minutes, stop by a museum or gallery, and sit in front of the first object or painting that resonates with you. Transport yourself. Drown out everything else around you. You'll return to your day's tasks much more focused. It will give you a completely different perspective and generally one that's much healthier.

My love for art began when I was seven years old. My parents sent me and my sister to MoMA, where they had painting classes for children. The curators who taught were so passionate about what they did that it really stuck. I remember painting great bursts of color, and imagining my paintings hanging in a museum. We would tour the museum as well; abstract expressionist pieces spoke to me the most because of the bold color fields.

I also collected all through childhood: Corgi cars, stamps, coins, travel posters. I began truly collecting art, however, when I was still in my teens. My grandfather had set up a small fund for me the day I was born, and I was told that it would be given to me when I turned eighteen. I was certain I wanted to spend it on art, so I started looking in galleries when I was seventeen. Most kids would probably have bought a car, taken a trip, or spent it on clothes. But instead I thought I would buy art.

I vividly remember buying my first piece. I went to a Christie's auction and bought a 1920s Jules Pascin watercolor. It was of an odalisque. It cost practically all the money my grandfather had given me, but I didn't care. I thought about what the picture said to me: the woman was so beautiful, and her beauty was conveyed by the most delicate brush strokes. I kept it for about ten years, and it formed the core of my early collection, but I wanted more art. I needed to surround it with pieces that related.

I worked two months of every summer in New York, and I would literally save every paycheck for art. I worked for a bond house as a runner on Wall Street, and as a messenger for a law firm. Not eating lunch for an entire year also helped; I put that money toward art, too. I wasn't following specific artists at that point per se. I would just buy whatever spoke to me that I could afford. A major gallery's owner even took a liking to me because I was a young kid with a passion, and he allowed me to buy pieces on layaway! I bought things at art fairs in Greenwich Village or the Hamptons, I went to London and bought art displayed on the fences of Hyde Park. Anything that sparked a positive response.

Only later, after I'd studied art history at Hobart College and I was in my very early twenties, did I begin to focus on particular artists and particular schools of art. This new education of course made me feel that my collection was not as interesting as I had thought at first. Luckily I had the eye to have purchased some fairly significant—for a young man—paintings and drawings that I could sell. It was my first foray into de-accessoning things that no longer spoke to me as they once had. Tastes evolve. Don't be afraid to admit that yours has, and to act on that realization by reinventing your collection or surroundings.

Affinity exists between art of different eras. A Mark Rothko, above left, and a folk art portrait by Ammi Phillips, above right, both share a ghostly air and a similar vision of proportion and line. Cohler finds them quintessentially American and has been inspired by them to incorporate large, flat areas of unbroken, muted color in his interiors.

Cohler sees architectural elements in John Singer Sargent's portrait, *Madame X*, 1883–84, left. Her stature is depicted as upright and proud yet carefully detailed and approachable—qualities Cohler believes all good buildings share. The curved facade of the diner in Edward Hopper's *Night-hawks*, 1942, above right, grounds and defines the social, human element in the painting; a similar architectural line in a client's foyer, right, inspired Cohler to arrange artwork by Frank Stella, Louise Nevelson, and Jean Dubuffet in a way that helped them to "converse" as well.

Elie Nadelman's sculpture, above, receives a custom-built display ledge made from nero assoluto granite, to set off its form and material. Similarly, white-lacquered walls help to highlight the intricate, curved details on a Louise Nevelson sculpture, right. Previous pages: A mirrored wall and furniture arranged away from a living room's artwork help guests appreciate it from many vantage points in the room. A tabletop stabile by Alexander Calder completes the grouping.

Interior Design, Art, Architecture, and Fashion All Relate

The great designers of the twentieth century all shared one particular trait: fearlessness. Philip Johnson is a classic example. There's a great anecdote about a visitor to his iconic Glass House. A guest said to him: "I couldn't live here." Johnson, who was very strongly opinionated and who was not in the least insecure, retorted: "No one's asking you to." He designed a house that worked for him, and he didn't care what other people thought about it. I tell all my clients this story because I want them to take the lesson to heart—what works for someone else isn't necessarily right for you.

There are many examples of fearless people who are admired. Elsie de Wolfe painted brown furniture white, Billy Baldwin used pattern on pattern, and David Hicks used color in abundance and mixed disparate objects. They were secure enough to express their personal style anywhere and everywhere. Fashion designers, furniture designers, artists, architects—the best of them are always fearless. Look to any of these disciplines for inspiration and ideas for your own interiors. So many people feel confident dressing

Cohler surrounded by a carefully grouped collection of some of his favorite art and furnishings, left, designed to "tailor" the room both to the apartment's architecture and his personality. Christian Dior's Bar Suit, above left, infamous for using an excessive amount of fabric during a time of privation immediately following World War II, and Babe Paley, above right, both exude elegance, clarity, structure, and mystery—qualities Cohler strives to incorporate into all his interiors projects.

themselves and buying property, but when it comes to interior design or art, they get nervous about making choices. Look at what you already own in other areas and think about what detail of your favorite pair of shoes, say, or your favorite dresses speak to you. Are they flashy? Subdued? Preppy? Casual? Formal? Maybe everything you own is striped. Translate that same look into your interiors, and they will come across with a surety of purpose—carry your vision out regardless of others' reactions. You know when what you've done suits you. Being able to make confident decisions puts you in the category of what I call "fabulous people."

If you consider yourself a pop culture fiend, watch your favorite music video online, or watch your favorite movie again and think about why its visual effects put you in a good mood. Is it set at the beach? Does it take place in a swell art deco hotel from the 1930s? Is it somber? Dissect it and capture some of those same elements in the objects that surround you every day.

Personally, I love art more than anything. When I look at the pieces of art in my collection, at the different photographs, I constantly come up with new ideas for clients. I see new things in the art each time I look at it; it's not merely wallpaper. I keep much of it in storage in a warehouse in Queens, and I go look at it when I need inspiration. I keep it relatively accessible so it can be easily pulled out. A few times a year I go and have

all 600 pieces set up around a large room and I spend several hours looking at them, taking notes, thinking about them, about what I'm seeing and about how it relates to how I want my clients' spaces to feel and to look. I concentrate and imagine that I can almost feel the artist's hand, what it took to produce a given work of art. I take something away from the experience, and that brush with pure creativity fuels me. It gives me a sense that I, too, can be creative for someone else by giving him or her a great palette for his or her home. It also gets me thinking about other, similarly themed items—art from a certain museum, or to a pattern, fabric, or color. This process is merely a sidebar to what I do every day, but it's my own form of meditation. Take something you are passionate about and listen to what it's telling you. It will guide you.

Monticello, Thomas Jefferson's Virginia home, above, features a European arrangement of artwork known as "salon style." He replicated the look after having visited private homes on the Continent. Inspired by Jefferson's parlor, a similar configuration of art, right—hung on airline-grade steel cable instead of brass hooks—serves as a solution for showcasing a collection in a contemporary apartment that has more windows than wall space.

Harmony between the oval motif on an abstract Jacob Kainen painting and the backs of
Swedish chairs reupholstered with brown suede, left, helps imbue a dining room with a
timeless, eclectic feel. Walls painted the color of tobacco and an English pine dining table
from the mid-nineteenth century add neutrality, and a light fixture inspired by T. H. Robsjohn-
Gibbings completes the ensemble. A vignette, above, featuring a Chinese vase, fifteenth-
century Korean earthenware sculpture, small wheat grass plant, and a lightbox filled with
vintage photographs continues the apartment's theme of décor from disparate eras.

Three paintings grouped for their similarly blocky style, above, grace the entry and small wall behind a custom headboard in a master bedroom. An antique *secrétaire à abattant* fills a niche on a landing perfectly, left. The addition of a Regency-style chair handpainted with a Greek key motif transforms the awkward space into a usable one.

Even a small master bedroom, above, can hold a bounty of the owner's personal treasures. A folding elephant-mounting ladder from India doubles as a library ladder here, two small-scale landscapes by Wolf Kahn fit just above the dresser, and a lime-green painting by Alex Katz adds a pop of color at an unexpected height—at eye level for someone sitting in an armchair. The narrow sitting area in the same suite, right, holds plenty of black-and-white photography; an eighteenth-century French limestone-topped ironwork table and a Louis XIII–style armchair covered in white linen add a sense of history to the small space.

It's Only Good Taste if
It Suits the Way You Live

I don't care if a client has good taste as long as he or she has a point of view. One of Diana Vreeland's great classic pronouncements sums it up: "Have good taste, have bad taste, just don't have no taste." What I help clients do is shape a point of view and sharpen it to bring out the essence of what they really want to have—versus what they would have done on their own. If the client has no point of view, it's a disaster. I can try to educate them as much as possible, but if I cannot instill passion, that's where we get into trouble. If the client doesn't have a point of view, even if they have bad taste, they don't have a sense of who they are and it's guaranteed they will never be satisfied with what I present. So clients have to come to me with at least a sense of departure. I can give them ideas, but they have to be receptive to them.

One of the first things I try to impress upon all my clients is this: nothing you have in your home should be so expensive or rare that you're afraid to use it. If everything in a room is of extremely high value, the whole room will feel completely flat. Anybody can go and spend a lot of money on furniture and put it together, but that's not creating a home. A client once said to me, "I want the typical Park Avenue apartment living room. I want my furniture grouped that way everyone else on Park Avenue has it." I looked at the man and asked, "What does that mean?" It was an absurd comment. I encouraged him to mix it up a little bit, to instill some personality and to suit his actual lifestyle, but he was so afraid of having his friends think what he did was wrong that he was willing to live uncomfortably. And so we parted ways.

There's a fine nuance between style and taste. Unlike style, which is mostly intrinsic and unique, what most people consider good taste can be learned. It's very safe and calm, and it's based on balance and harmony. It looks and feels good. Taste can be manufactured. It's choosing from a menu of options, but choosing wisely. The components of taste are mass-produced. When you go to a design center, for example, you are choosing from ready-made items that can sometimes be customized. My favorite analogy is that it's like cooking from a recipe. True chefs, as we know, cook from instinct. Regarding interior design, begin by taking small steps toward individuality. Think of it as putting tomatoes on your Caesar salad. You know you didn't invent the Caesar salad, but within reasonable parameters, you can make it your own.

**Design considerations are subservient to what works best
for a client's existing art collection in a modern loft, right.
The entry hall and living room are kept to a neutral palette
so as not to distract from the abstract art's bold forms.**

Panoramic views of downtown New York City serve as dynamic wallpaper when seen through floor-to-ceiling windows, left. Custom drapes with Greek key trim, a vintage Danish modern chaise, and a simple black iron floor lamp are all the fittings the space requires to feel complete. Overleaf: In a living room, custom blond wood paneling conceals structural elements left raw by the building's developer. Low-intensity beige and blue tones on the furniture and sisal carpet keep the space feeling light-filled and relaxing per the clients' request, and relate to the building's cast-glass window frames.

Ten chairs by Cherner grace a long dining table that accentuates the generous length of the apartment's public rooms, above. A custom light fixture by Mark Figueredo mimics the varying heights of the buildings in the cityscape visible just outside the windows. A small, custom-designed kitchen island, right, adds functional counter space to the room without breaking up the visual line in the apartment's open-plan living areas—an important feature for the clients, who love to entertain and interact with guests while meals are being prepared.

Fanciful patterns in vibrant-but-unexpected colors grace a girl's room, above. Circular motifs unite the fabrics on the draperies and bedding, and a custom headboard adds a decidedly feminine touch. Simple Artemide swing-arm lamps are repurposed as sturdy sconces. Blues and browns reign in a boy's room, opposite. The casual midcentury furniture, built-in storage, and mature color scheme will remain appropriate as the inhabitant matures. Previous pages: A master bedroom proves that contemporary does not have to be equated with "cold." Thick color-blocked drapes begin the motif of cozy, relaxing hues that define the space. Accent colors of warm spring green appear on the chaise, armchair, and custom bedding to give the ensemble depth.

S hopping only from design centers or catalogs allows someone to dictate to you how you should live, what you should wear, what you should sit on. It's all done with predigested, good taste. They're convenient, but by nature they're meant to appeal to the Everyman. For something truly special, be willing to risk making a few mistakes. You'll certainly have more fun along the way and you'll feel more proud of your home.

The definition of bad taste is very subjective. I consider bad taste to be terrible color choices, too much pattern, or too much fabric on the windows—anytime you feel like you're suffocating in a room or that something is really missing, it qualifies as bad. People tend to hang a picture smack in the middle of a wall, with nothing around to anchor it, so it's unconnected. But who's to say it's not in good taste? In my professional opinion, it's not. I think it's better to hang pictures in a way that encourages you to engage with the art, rather than feel like you have to admire it from afar, stiffly, like in a white-cube art gallery.

Bad taste isn't necessarily a lack of taste—it may be a lack of conventional taste. It's very easy for someone who's a designer to be a bit of a snob and say to himself about a space, "Well, this is dreadful—what am I going to do with *this*?" But the person who lives there may love each and every object, so you have to respect that. Bad taste can have a point of view that legitimizes it. Take Archie Bunker's living room in *All in the Family* as an example. That room is really in bad taste. But at least it was *his* room and it matched his personality. It reflected the way he wanted to live. The same is true for the set of *I Love Lucy*. It may not be necessarily what you think of as good taste—but it reflected the characters who lived there. The way a person lives in his or her own home is the only thing that matters. If you can sense the strength of a person's character from the décor, even if it's in an environment you would never choose for yourself, it's legitimate. It's his or her idea of heaven.

This is an important point: nothing is in good taste unless it suits the way you live. If it resonates with you, then it qualifies as good taste. Even if it's a chartreuse living room. People who entertain often, in particular, seem to convince themselves that there's a certain way a room should look to make it seem well behaved. They want a room to be "the proper yellow" instead of their favorite color, with crown moldings, furniture covered in chenille fabric with small patterns, or whatever the masses or the shelter magazine cabal deems is "in" at the moment. But it's not a proper living room if it doesn't suit you and make you happy.

Editing and weeding through the things you already have helps bring clarity to a space. Think of it as pruning, the way a gardener creates a landscape out of unruly plants. Take everything off your display

A Massimo Vitali beach photograph lends itself to furnishings and accessories reminiscent of summertime fun. An acrylic klismos chair with a vibrant seat vies for attention with an Arne Jacobsen Egg chair covered in a highly graphic fabric while a mirrored console table and custom chrome-and-glass coffee table by John Boone bounce sunlight through the space.

Six Donald Judd prints reign
over a room designed to be
family friendly but still chic,
left. John Saladino's clear
table lamps keep sight lines
to the outside open for
people gathered on a
sectional sofa covered in
chocolate-brown mohair.
Overleaf: A horse portrait
by Roberto Dutesco is paired
simply with a Flat Bar Brno
chair covered in brown
leather, top left. A metal
chest by Andrew Martin,
near top right, adds an
industrial note and reflects
the carpet's vibrant pattern-
ing. A gaming area, far right,
features a custom table with
pull-out drink holders.

shelves, then put each object back one by one, looking at it for shape and to decide how much you actually love it. Since possessions tend to amass slowly over time, evaluating your belongings in one sitting can reveal a lot. Clear yourself a clean landscape, but remember to include a few "shrubs" with an unusual form to torque it so it's not too perfect.

Sometimes bad taste can be exciting. You may have too many of grandma's Hummel figurines clustered on every surface because you happened to inherit them. You probably don't truly love them, but they have some sentimental value and you can't bring yourself to throw them away. Maybe you can pick one incredible Hummel figure that you know you just have to keep, and put it smack dab in the middle of the mantel next to a truly nice crystal sculpture. Because it's so antithetical to the other objects, it might work. It becomes profane. Ironic.

Even worse than bad taste is no taste. Think of the typical college dorm: a bed without a headboard, white walls, two end tables with two matching lamps, a storage bolster covered in faux leather. And the rugs are wall-to-wall nylon carpet. There's no art on the walls at all. There's a large television that takes up half the room. The windows have miniblinds on them, or nothing. That's it. When you go into a space like that—

but at someone's home—you ask yourself what kind of person could possibly live there. Spaces that lack any outward evidence of personal investment make you feel like you're walking into a nightmarish Kafka novel.

I also find it stifling and shocking that people can live in a place where they haven't had the inspiration, guts, or chutzpah to add even a *single* personal object. No dog-eared novels on shelves, no family photographs, nothing to describe the person who lives there. To me that's no taste. It's banal, invisible. And it's anathema to everything I try to achieve as a designer. To figure these people out, I have to put on my shrink hat and very nicely try to analyze how they feel about their own home. Then we can tweak it a bit to create a sense of security, or a sense of cosseted luxury. Even if this sounds like you, the good news is that once you take the time to personalize, you'll feel better. Every single day.

Walnut cabinets in a custom-designed kitchen, above, relate to the apartment's overall color scheme and relaxed-yet-cosmopolitan mood. The space's breakfast nook, right, features contemporary furnishings such as a custom banquette, Philippe Starck's Ghost chair, and a David Weeks light fixture. Art by the clients' children is on proud display.

Scalloped forms unite two custom furnishings in a girl's room. A headboard, above, features a bold print with accents of orange-red, a color picked up on a graphic settee, right. Curtains close around the space to give her a cozy, private reading area.

Yes, It's All Right to
Incorporate Off-the-Shelf Items

One of the most successful rooms I've ever seen was designed by Mark Hampton for Anne Bass. It mixed art by Rothko with truly wonderful English Georgian furniture all covered in one color, kind of an off-white, creamy, lineny hue. The room was anchored simply with a beautiful Aubusson rug. Covering all the furniture in one fabric simplified it and kept it from feeling fussy or heavy. It actually feels light and ethereal—in just the same way the Rothkos are ethereal. It was a brilliant move, and allowed contemporary, midcentury, world-class art to live happily with antique furniture. Most people would never have put them together, but they play off each other, and the furniture seems to float in the room.

Reproduction furniture is different because it's made with a commercial bent; the focus is on pleasing the masses. The object of designing it is purely to make money. Using newly made furniture exclusively in a room, however, makes a space fall flat as far as I'm concerned. Save space for one or two amazing accents.

A knockoff is something that is never the same as the original—the lines are slightly altered, the proportion is different, the texture is not the same. You can buy a look-alike Eero Saarinen table, but it just won't feel quite right. If you take it as a starting point, though, and you alter it in a way that makes it your own, that's acceptable and encouraged! Artists do this all the time; so do fashion designers. Appropriate a reproduction, but do it in a way that makes you reinvent it and put your own moniker on it. We can't all be Coco Chanel, but we can still wear interesting tweeds.

Personalized touches make a room couture. Even if an object's pedigree is less than blue-blooded, if it has an unusual or eye-catching shape, snap it up. You can order a catalog sofa that will cost $15,000 because of how it's built and the manufacturer's name. You might think you have something great, and in reality it's probably unremarkable. But if you take a cheaper model and have it covered in a bold fabric you found on a trip abroad, people will notice that it's unique, not that its cushions are made of compacted foam instead of springs. It will be much more memorable and admired. I promise.

Interior designers are often called upon to decorate model apartments like the one at right, which demand the use of easy-to-source, inexpensive, off-the-shelf furnishings; but the end result of any space filled with reasonably priced items or fittings need not be boring if a little ingenuity is used. Checkered grass cloth wallpaper in the foyer relates to the interlocking square shapes on the rug beyond, while a simple painted border along the ceiling gives the space a bespoke touch.

Also remember that the mix is better than the match. Buying too many pieces from any one source or from any single time period makes a space feel bland. You don't live in a historical novel—why try to literally dwell in the past? One of my clients spent $6,000 on six lovely, Regency-era dining room chairs we found on a trip abroad—a significant percentage of her overall budget. So when we got home, we went to Crate and Barrel and bought a simple table on sawhorse legs for $900. The unexpected pairing gave the room a *frisson* that was very successful. There's almost no design problem that can't be solved with a little ingenuity, and budgetary constraints can actually prompt you to be more creative.

Mixing items from several producers helps to achieve a curated feeling. In a living room, above, a brown-and-white pillow from Pottery Barn mixes with a low white drink table and club chairs from West Elm; the Barcelona stool in front of the fireplace is a reproduction. A pair of Tang Dynasty terra-cotta horses and sconces by Jean de Merry add luxurious touches. A kitchen and dining area, opposite, are fitted with tableware from CB2; the lamp is Artemide and the dining chairs are replicas of Danish modern originals. Ceilings are papered and painted for dimension, and solar shades on the windows modulate harsh light to help the developer-standard room feel cocooning.

Simply altering one detail of an off-the-shelf item can help it feel customized. Above, panel curtains receive simple trim, a Blu Dot sofa's back cushion is removed to help it better relate to the scale of the apartment, a side chair from HB Home is given a horsehair cushion, and a basic square ottoman receives a fun orange cover. Carefully chosen catalog items, left, make an entry hall feel well-appointed. The console table and resin horn sculpture are from Flair, the hurricane from Pottery Barn. The space's one truly luxurious element is an Hermès tray. Previous pages: Graphic pop gives a room all the personality it needs. The rug, from Beauvais, is the space's most attention-getting element, and therefore receives the biggest slide of the budget. Zebra curtains are made of Cohler's fabric for Lee Jofa, the simple sofas are by Max&Co., and a pair of bobbin chairs are given a white-linen facelift to fit in with the room's casual atmosphere.

A wall lined simply in fabric, right, adds ample richness to an otherwise straightforward guest bedroom. The four-poster iron bed, bedside lamps, and settee are from Max&Co., the bedding from Williams-Sonoma Home. Previous pages: Patterned damask grass cloth wallpaper from Phillip Jeffries adds an opulent touch to a master bedroom fitted with a bed by Jonathan Adler, bedding by Restoration Hardware, and Bungalow 5 side tables. Hand-painted Regency mirrors add a touch of history that keeps the space feeling authentic.

CHAPTER IV

LIVE WITH WHAT YOU LOVE

Too many of us live in homes or apartments that don't feel connected to our lifestyles. We primarily spend time in the bedroom, in the kitchen, or around a television in a family gathering space. Most people rarely use a living room—it's virtually become a misnomer—let alone sit down to meals in a dining room. I ask clients when we first meet *how* they live. This is a simple needs analysis; if they tell me they entertain only at the holidays, or if I discover they're using formal rooms half a dozen times a year maximum, I try to convince them that they don't need them. That's valuable real estate—especially in a city, but an unused dining room in a large suburban or country home is also great space that could be put to better use. Being honest with yourself about how you like to live is paramount; forget conventional ideas about the rooms you think a house "should" have. Guests will always be more comfortable in an authentic space with personality than in a stuffy "proper" room, and so will you.

I once turned a dining room into a billiard room. If a pool table animates your space and would make you spend more time in it, adding one would be a good decision. Why not fit the table with a removable top, so you can use it as a dining room on holidays? Or let a dining room become another bedroom or an office—it doesn't need to be static. The same holds true for the living room; create a library instead if it means you will use it more: build a banquette into a corner coupled with a square or round table that's extendable for entertaining and line the walls with shelves for books and family photos. Anchor the room with a television and overscaled bean bags. Perhaps it sounds inelegant, but I guarantee your family will gravitate to the space, making the unorthodox decision completely justifiable. It's a convenient, cozy space for kids to do their homework, for you to use a laptop or read.

**Larry Charles's painting *Pink Horizon on Black Ground*
and a Burmese sculpture purchased during a trip
imbue a living room with deep personal meaning.**

The same advice applies to the kitchen. Galley kitchens, with a balanced layout—a "work triangle" between sink, stove, and refrigerator—are the most efficient. They keep us from having to walk around and around an oversized island; that's why restaurants use them. Today's kitchens are trending larger, but the actual workspace should be small in size and well planned. Having prep materials easily at hand is more of an everyday luxury than pot racks overhead you can't reach or built-in plate racks that look attractive but only hold plates that are "too nice" for everyday use. I'm an advocate of using what you have. Why save it? Take your wedding china off the shelf and serve dinner on it—your children probably won't want to inherit it anyway, they will want to choose their own pattern. The same applies to silver flatware. Treat yourself, even if that means polishing it more often. Devote the remainder of the kitchen to family space or entertaining space.

Express your inner decorative fantasies in your rooms, your own sense of how you want a space to look, how you want to live. This will help endow them with style as well as function. If you want a room that's reflective of your own style compass, think about incorporating elements that are not on the "menu" in catalogs or online. Create a space that will become uniquely yours. Just as Parisian fashions are copied every season and distilled down to the lowest common denominator of "style" for the mass market, many modern furniture companies present you with images of complete rooms that you can buy just by picking up the phone or with the click of a mouse. However, caveat emptor! Just as you would never buy all your clothes from one designer for fear of looking the same all the time, you should never buy all of your furniture from one or two sources, lest the room look boring and bromidic.

A critical lesson to remember: personal style isn't about going out and buying the most expensive carpets, furniture, or fabrics: it is about being able to arrange a few interesting pieces next to inexpensive pieces. Mix them in with your family's collection, with quirky things that truly express your inner self. Live with what you love.

Small vignettes of personal mementos add depth to any interior. A trompe l'œil watercolor, a torso by Anita Huffington, and an intricately detailed box catch the eye in a library, right.

Give Every Room Character

Don't let shelter magazines and catalogs convince you that you need every interior to be too perfect. Interiors must be slightly torqued, askew. Why? Because life is that way. Not everything should be lined up as if in a showroom—looking stilted and artificial. What might be considered a design faux pas technically can make a room much warmer, more inviting, more comfortable, and ultimately more livable. We revere rooms created by David Hicks, Billy Baldwin, Dorothy Draper, even—gulp—Sister Parish; they are memorable because they express a true point of view, a strong personality. Start thinking about your own interiors by looking to some of the past's most admired iconoclasts, not merely at safe, "tasteful" publications. Shelter magazines are tremendously informative and educational, but try not to make them the only reference tool in your design library.

Too many interiors that we see promoted are spaces that it's unlikely you're going to look at in five, ten, or twenty years and say, "That's an amazing room." You're going to look back and say, "That's so dated." If a design is not a well thought out modern reinterpretation of a classic style, it's just a rehash. Tear pages out of a magazine that catch your eye; maybe a staircase detail based on a traditional Chippendale railing or an interesting design motif on a fabric that's a classic suzani design exploded and made much larger. Be influenced by the past, but shake it up a little.

In the 1950s and 1960s American designers were creating truly fresh looks ceaselessly. Knoll stands out as one of the most innovative companies of the era. There seemed to be more reverence for imagination then. We've been culturally programmed to support our own efforts at mass production, to the detriment of true artisans. We could use a healthy dose of appreciation for what the Japanese call *wabi sabi*—an aesthetic that believes imperfection is beauty and that promotes a respect for things that are used, transient, incomplete.

What is sublime isn't something you've found online, it's a room that functions as your own catalog—of places you've visited, people you've loved, colors that move you, furniture that fits your lifestyle. It's about balancing overtly beautiful items with funny little pieces that speak to you. A truly successful room is infused with duality, texture, originality, and verve!

Faces on Fornasetti wallpaper and a Chippendale chair from the eighteenth century recovered with David Hicks fabric greet visitors to an entry hall. Overleaf left: Black crown molding adds drama to a sitting room and helps the graphics of a Nell Blaine etching pop. Overleaf right: A nineteenth-century Danish portrait and a Frances Elkins footstool designed for the Tobin Clark estate add a historic feeling to the room's straightforward architecture.

An intimate seating area furnished with casually slipcovered Lee Jofa club chairs, above, receives a jolt of formality from a diminutive English travel desk, the first laptop. Layered framed works— photography, painting, and works on paper—and a sculpture create a rich vignette on a console table, adding interest to a corner of the room. Overleaf left: Colors and curves unite an abstract work by David Slivka, a painting by Alex Katz, a Chinese terra-cotta camel, a folk art sculpture, and modern candleholder; an eighteenth-century Swedish console table forms the base. Overleaf right: Silver-leaf wallpaper by Phillip Jeffries adds glimmer to a dining room covered in oxblood paint. A Beauvais rug and traditional Indonesian basket add texture to the space.

Trompe l'œil hand-painted walls by Cole and Son give
undeniable personality to a dressing room, above,
guaranteed to invigorate its owner each and every morning.

Contrast creates coziness in a bedroom. A papier-maché deer head silhouetted against a dark wall draws the eye to a ceiling covered in grass cloth, above, while a mantel designed by Mario Buatta holds an assortment of personal treasures. Art placed above a tufted, custom headboard, right, relates to the scale of its sections; a hand-painted lamp by Timothy Brown, a linen-and-nailhead side table, and a suzani throw continue the dark-and-light scheme.

Torque the Details

Sometimes people hire a designer because they're trying to acquire a look they associate with "old money." They try to live up to an imagined picture of interiors that they have aspired to and can now afford to create. Rooms designed under this pretext are nothing more than stage sets. These aren't rooms that invite you to sit down and enjoy yourself, or to have a drink and be able to set it down without having to worry about leaving condensation rings on a priceless antique. They're supposed to be the epitome of hospitality, but really they're not hospitable at all; they are moribund and lack character. In high school, I was once sitting with a friend from a well-known family. She propped her feet up on a beautiful lacquer coffee table in her parents' Fifth Avenue living room. I was aghast. When I asked whether her mom would be mad, she laughed, saying, "No. We only keep things we can afford to replace." That was that, so I swung my feet, shoes and all, onto the table too. Lesson learned.

Anybody can spend a lot of money on furniture. A client literally once said to me, "I want the typical 'Park Avenue apartment' living room." It was an absurd comment. I no longer work with that client because I just couldn't reconcile myself to giving him something that wouldn't reflect any of his own personality. He had the money to afford wonderful art, artisan-made furniture, and unusual fabrics, but he didn't want to work to include any memorable or imaginative details. What a shame.

You don't need to hire a designer to get the look of a "classic" Park Avenue living room. Here's why: all you need are two settees facing each other in front of a fireplace crowned with a trumeau mirror, a grand piano in a corner, and a large overstuffed sofa against one wall with a Chinese Coromandel screen behind it. Add a couple of lamps, Louis XVI or Gustavian tables, an oriental rug, and a pair of bridgewater armchairs and *voilà*.

I would much rather work with a client who said, "Give me a chartreuse living room." Maybe people *would* come over and say to themselves, "Oh my God . . . a chartreuse living room." But at least it would be fun. And at the end of the day it's your house, so who cares what other people think if you're the one who has to live there and it makes you happy? If you have one wild concept or wall color in mind to use as a catalyst, indulge yourself but temper the room. Let one strong statement energize the space rather than trying to interject too many lively pieces, like a purple sofa in one corner, a mauve chair in another, and an orange coffee table—I've seen it!

A few small objets, such as an Anita Huffington torso sculpture and glass bowl filled with decorative balls add interest to a coffee table, all of which are reflected in an antique convex mirror for extra impact.

Greek keys, one of Cohler's favorite motifs, are used as details on a mantel he designed for Chesney's, in the United Kingdom, left, and a settee for Lee Jofa, above. Overleaf left: Custom paneling conceals electronic equipment to keep an interior consistent with its house's traditional architecture; a Regency convex mirror provides a foil to the highly rectilinear forms.

A quoined corner and a custom-designed exterior light, above, add personality to the exterior of a house in Connecticut. A light well, flanked by lightning rods decorated with blue glass bulbs, opens onto guest quarters on a house's interior, right.

A pool house, right and overleaf, provides extensive indoor/outdoor living and entertaining areas; a screen at the pool's opposite end can be rolled up and down for outdoor movie showings.

Contemporary and antique furniture mix happily in a lively kitchen and dining area that can open wide to the yard beyond. A deeply recessed tray ceiling and skylight bring light deep into the casual interior.

Dare to Be Daring

Decorator show houses allow interior designers an unfettered opportunity to experiment with interiors; they serve as design labs. In reality a client might not choose to live in a show house room—but they might want to incorporate an element extracted from one. These rooms may look great in and of themselves, or be eye-catching if reproduced in the glossy pages of a magazine or online, but you probably would not want to live in a space where each and every element was designed to be flashy; these rooms are very theatrical. The best show house rooms are those where the designer has envisioned a real person he or she knows, and has imagined him or her living there. Not posturing too hard, but pushing the envelope just enough to give visitors the idea that being daring is a good thing. The most successful and memorable show house rooms are those where you walk in and hear people saying, "I could really live here." The rooms look real. Show houses give designers free rein to try out schemes they've had percolating in the backs of their minds and, while they're usually saturated with many design ideas at once because the amount of space the designers get is limited to one room, they can be great places to pick up a slightly audacious idea and try it at home.

Billy Baldwin's classic interior for Mr. and Mrs. Lee Eastman, left, with its deeply colored, reflective walls and use of large-scale art inspired Cohler's 2010 room for New York's Holiday House, right, a show house benefitting breast cancer research. Overleaf: The room's high-gloss lacquered boiserie, silver-leaf wallpaper ceiling, and pair of Regency parcel gilt mirrors keep the light from a Giacometti floor lamp, vintage glass-and-brass ceiling fixture, and pair of sconces cascading vibrantly. Jayne Wrightsman dining chairs are upholstered in Cohler's Dinesen fabric for Lee Jofa; the room's other main pattern is provided by the custom-designed, pagoda-style valances and draperies in a graphic black-and-white print.

For Holiday House's 2009 room, themed "Father's Day," above and right, Cohler hand painted the wooden floor in a graphic black-and-white design inspired by David Hicks and added further chrome-and-black accent pieces throughout, such as a sawhorse desk and throw pillows in two patterns. Six photos from the *New York Times* collection surround a larger shot. Overleaf: Masculine touches, such as a model sailboat hung on cables to display as sculpture, cubic lanterns of Cohler's design, an embossed faux-crocodile ceiling covering, and a pair of Regency armchairs upholstered in black patent leather define the space. The yellow sofa grounds the room with a pop of color.

If It Looks Right, It Is Right

Luxury can be many things. It's not necessarily about having the most expensive rug, the rarest chair, or bedroom walls lined with cashmere. It's about finding a balance between aesthetic pleasure and feeling comfortable.

To me, luxury is coming home to a true haven at the end of the day, where living is easy and the things you need are close at hand. A lavish detail or two can help to instill this mood or make a daily routine go more smoothly, certainly, but few people really feel relaxed in a room full of precious, fussy things. There needs to be a balance between visual considerations and intuitive design. Say you're in bed and you want to have a sip of water—if your bespoke nightstand has a tray that pulls out to help you reach it, that's luxury. Or perhaps you have swing-arm sconces mounted on the wall to either side of your headboard so you don't have to crowd the surface of your nightstand with a lamp, but can use it for books, an iPad, or laptop. This is a simple and practical luxurious touch, too.

Being able to put things into a place where they feel natural and intuitive—while looking good—represents the ideal for luxurious interior design. Luxury is about integrating small things to help you get through your day, help you achieve personal harmony, help make your house "a machine for living," as Le Corbusier said. Spaces within your home should make you feel good—they should be personalized, and make you feel cosseted and surrounded by a certain air of calm. Make wherever you call home your family's refuge.

Dorothy Draper, left, is known for her many witty maxims on the rules of interior design. "If it looks right, it is right," one of her most famous, inspired Cohler as he worked to design a relatively small Miami condominium around a client's vibrant art collection and make the many worthy pieces sit well together.

A haunting portrait by Alex Katz greets visitors in an entryway, right. Overleaf: A large-scale painting by Jean-Michel Basquiat and an Alexander Calder mobile grace the living room; beige upholstery references the beachside location and allows the art to take center stage while the iron bases of a coffee table and campaign stool echo the painting's deep background color.

In a sitting room, tables purchased on a trip to London inject hits of brown also picked up in a Robert Rauschenberg painting over the sofa; a small John Chamberlain sculpture rests in the foreground.

Surprising harmony results when a George Condo painting, above and right, is paired with a traditionally patterned Oriental rug in a sympathetic color palette. A Fernando Botero sculpture's gleaming, dark surface is also reflected in klismos dining chairs covered with ostrich leather.

CHAPTER V

THE PAST IS PROLOGUE

I need to be inspired by the past to create a template for the future. When designing a new piece of furniture or a fabric, it's usually informed to some degree by history—either a vintage color, a shape popular in a certain century, or a texture that speaks to opulent materials seldom manufactured today. My designs always cross-pollinate with many disciplines; I'll often be inspired by something I've seen in one form and apply it to a different medium. The sleight of hand that makes this process "good design" is to create a finished whole. Mixing eras takes tremendous restraint. It's easy to have an interior with an eclectic collection turn out looking like all the ingredients were thrown into one big pot. It's far better to have a room unfold gradually and with intention, like a five-course meal.

I learned the hard way that it's just as important for me to interview clients before we agree to work together as it is for them to interview me. It has to be a good fit; they have to be receptive and acknowledge that their house should reflect the way they actually live—not the way they *think* they *should* be living. This is a seemingly simple point, but one that is overlooked or ignored surprisingly often. Keep it in mind. For example: What side of the bed do you sleep on? Don't arrange a room in a way that will force you to have to change sleeping where you're comfortable. Make your house fit your needs. These are often intimate questions, but they have to be thought through. They impact your lifestyle dramatically. Do you read late at night when your spouse wants to sleep? Be sure to arrange different lighting on one side of the bed from the other. Are you a watch-television-in-bed person? What size TV do you need so you'll be able to see it comfortably from across the room? Do you have a lot of shoes, handbags, suits? Write down your needs. These seemingly small considerations impact your lifestyle dramatically. You may not have realized that you weren't living in a way that makes your life easy until you focus on it. Regardless, use your own past as prologue to incorporate elements into your home that help you live the way you've always wished you could; but remember that what you can't do is live in a perfect dollhouse world that makes your daily life awkward and forced instead of easy and pleasant.

Nesting antique chairs and a stone Kouros sculpture embellish an octagonal foyer, above. Horizontally striped wallpaper mediates a double-height landing and stairwell, right, keeping the scale of a sitting area welcoming. Previous pages: Thomas Jefferson's Monticello inspired the architecture of a house in Sharon, Connecticut, that Cohler designed, particularly in the shapes of the clerestory windows, columns, and railing that lines the balcony.

Rich fabrics in graphic patterns that, while disparate, relate in tone define a seating area, above: a dining chair is covered in a traditional toile, an armchair in custom-designed linen shot through with ribbon, and a sofa in a modern graphic print. A thick sisal rug helps them blend. Blue Farrow & Ball wallpaper and a doorway based on an Irish Georgian pediment lend a period flavor to a dining room, right; chairs slipcovered in antique nineteenth-century linen add to the theme in a subtle way.

Every nook presents a fair opportunity for design. A nineteenth-century American architect's stool with a unique form and an abstract painting peek out from a small passageway, above. In a master bedroom, the traditional form of a four-poster bed is given an update with side curtain panels for privacy, right.

An antique American drop-leaf table is a subtle reference to history in a kitchen, above.
Klismos chairs covered in saddle-leather upholstery with nailhead detail and a banquette add
modern flair to the space. A small wet bar, left, is surrounded by lighting features that hark
to eras past but is fitted with custom cabinetry that keeps functionality firmly in the present.

It's not merely average people who have difficulty communicating what they need. Dominique de Menil, patron of the arts, and architect Philip Johnson thought they understood each other, and although he designed a house for her family in the late 1940s that was publicly renowned as an example of purity in domestic modernism, she was furious when she saw the completed structure; it was far too ascetic for her lifestyle. She had difficulty articulating to Johnson what it was she really wanted, and the architect clearly had his own strong ideas about how the house should look—a recipe for disaster. They didn't speak for a decade afterward.

Be your own best client: think about what you will have to implement in your home to help you live your life. Express a point of view. Decide what inspires you well in advance of contracting with a builder or decorator. Maybe you have a collection that you would like to incorporate in a more prominent way; maybe you can't seem to get lighting right. Do you need to block light but don't want blackout curtains? Do you have offbeat ideas about how to arrange furniture but don't know how to implement them?

The New York townhouse Cohler grew up in, second from right, above, informed his design of an Upper East Side townhouse just across the street he was later commissioned to renovate, right.

If you take the plunge and hire an interior designer, try to remember that he or she may develop ideas that you didn't think of—amazing things can happen if you're receptive. I once had a client with an apartment on Central Park West. He was a successful money manager, and because he was used to making solid business decisions and being in control, he thought he had all the answers about interior design as well. Every time my team suggested something, he would second-guess us. Eventually, he fired me and hired somebody else. Three months later he sent a note to say that he had made a serious mistake, and he should have kept us on. Although he was resistant to relinquishing control when we suggested it, he came to understand that we were right to be insistent. I had to tell another client, a plastic surgeon, to restrict herself to doing what she did best—taking care of patients. Once all parties agree on the interior's direction, let my team take over. A doctor would never give you an appendectomy on the left side instead of the right just because you thought the scar would be less noticeable that way, but doctors have made requests about design that sound, to us, equally absurd. Some things in interior design simply shouldn't be done, and for good reason. If you approach interior design and architecture with even parts preparation and open mind, however, the results should exceed your expectations.

Souvenirs from the owners' tours of Europe lend a historic feeling to a classically designed townhouse, above and left. Intaglios, busts, architectural fragments and miniatures, jasperware, and bronzes pepper the space. A Donald Sultan photograph of smoke rings, above the fireplace, adds a contemporary twist.

Architectural engravings and small busts arranged on a console are elements of traditional decoration that draw the visitor into a library, left. A Syrie Maugham–style custom tufted headboard in a master bedroom, above, and a bench with antique French bronze legs keep the space feeling classic while Paul McCobb side tables add a small midcentury modern touch.

Acknowledgments

I've always believed that the first rule of success in any field is the understanding that it's "we," never "me." *Cohler on Design* could not have been possible without a team effort; an effort put forth by friends, family, staff, clients, colleagues, vendors, editors, and publishers. Among these I'd like to single out:

Michelle Keith, for it was she that led me to the first door, a door opened by Stacee Gravelle Lawrence and Gianfranco Monacelli.

Kelly Boyett, for her patience and dedication despite my having driven her slightly mad on several occasions.

Doug Turshen and Steve Turner for making the firm look so good on paper, and Mikhaela Mahony for patiently sorting out image rights.

Tony Klein, Jennifer Mason, and Helene Summa for helping turn the creative kernel of dreams into reality. Michael Fey for always being there; and our entire staff for their unique ability to create beauty anywhere—interior design takes vision and they are extraordinary visionaries.

The photographers, especially Francis Smith, whose images in these pages depict more than a moment in time; they convey a lifestyle.

Our research assistants and archivists at Condé Nast, Hearst, and Meredith.

My cheerleaders among the press for their encouraging words and support, including: Michael Boodro, Dominique Browning, Dara Caponigro, Ann Maine, Marian McEvoy, Lisa Newsome, Margaret Russell, and Newell Turner.

Stephen Elrod for his singular guidance in helping me create fabric collections for Lee Jofa, and to the Kravet Family for believing.

Andy Singer of Visual Comfort, for giving me the opportunity to develop a lighting collection, and to Nancy Wekselbaum for the introduction.

Stephen Fanuka, Rory McReesh, Vicki Gorelik, Boris Abromivich, Jinpra, and the many stars who keep it all flowing behind the scenes.

Eileen and Peter Rhulen for that first chance.

All of our clients for their patronage, and for graciously letting us photograph their homes.

Hobart College; The Graduate School of Design at Harvard University; and the Department of Architecture, Preservation and Planning at Columbia University.

Sharon Baum and Pam Liebman of Corcoran, Sheila Ellis of Sotheby's International.

Realty, Louise Sunshine of Sunshine-Corcoran, and Steve Roth of Vornado.

Daphne Merkin, Ina Garten, and Stephen Drucker—brilliantly gifted all.

Photography Credits

© Stefano Amantini / Atlantide Phototravel / Corbis: 94 top

John Arthur: 96

Stacy Bass: 198–99, 200–201, 202–203

Photography by John Bessler. Reprinted with permission from *Traditional Home*® magazine. ©2009, Meredith Corporation. All rights reserved.: 193

Photography by John Bessler. Reprinted with permission from *Traditional Home*® magazine. ©2012, Meredith Corporation. All rights reserved.: 117 top, 118, 119 bottom

Steven Brooke Studios: 9, 123 bottom, 124–25, 126, 127, 213, 214–15, 216–17, 218–19, 220, 221

Courtesy Hearst: 204

Chicago History Museum, Film negatives HB-04781-P and HB-04781-V: 115 top and bottom

Chicago History Museum, Photographic print HB-04969-D: 114'

Christian Dior (1905–1957). Bar Suit, 1947. Silk jacket, wool skirt. Jacket: C.I.58.34.30; skirt: C.I.69.40. Gift of Mrs. John Chambers Hughes, 1958 (C.I.58.34.309); Gift of Christian Dior, 1969 (C.I.69.40). The Metropolitan Museum of Art, New York, New York. Image copyright © The Metropolitan Museum of Art. Image source: Art Resource.: 129 left

Darren Chung: 119 top

Courtesy Eric Cohler: 11, 72, 100, 101, 113, 121, 240

Photography by Colleen Duffley. Reprinted with permission from *Traditional Home*® magazine. ©2006 Meredith Corporation. All rights reserved.: 71

Roger Davies: 153, 154–55, 156 left, 156 right, 157, 158, 159, 160, 161

From the archives of Dorothy Draper & Co. Inc./New York, The Carleton Varney Design Group: 212

Pieter Estersohn: 93

Caspar David Friedrich (1774–1840). *Wanderer Above a Sea of Fog,* ca. 1817. Oil on canvas, 94.8 x 74.8 cm. Inv.: 5161. On permanent loan from the Foundation for the Promotion of the Hamburg Art Collections. Photo: Elke Walford/bpk, Berlin / Art Resource, New York: 50

William Geddes: 12, 15, 16 left, 16 right, 17, 18, 19, 22–23, 24, 25, 26, 27, 28–29, 97

Thomas Grimes: 232, 233, 234, 235, 236, 237

Jeffrey Hirsch: 128

Edward Hopper (1882–1967). *Nighthawks, 1942,* 1942. Oil on canvas. 33 1/8 x 60 in. (84.1 x 152.4 cm). Friends of American Art Collection, 1942.51. The Art Institute of Chicago.: 123 top

Horst P. Horst / ©Corbis: 129 right

© Michael Kim / Corbis: 92

Courtesy Kohler Co.: 94 bottom, 95

Johansen Krause: 224, 225, 226, 227, 229, 230, 231

Robert Lautman / Thomas Jefferson Foundation at Monticello: 130

John Lawrence: 117 bottom

Noni MacLeay: 194, 195 top left, 195 bottom left, 195 bottom right, 196, 197, 222 top, 222 bottom left

Mary Porter / Thomas Jefferson Foundation at Monticello: 222 bottom right

Mark Rothko / *Untitled (Black on Gray),* 1969/1970 / Acrylic on canvas / 80 1/8 x 69 1/8 inches (203.3 x 175.5 cm) / Solomon R. Guggenheim Museum, New York / Gift, The Mark Rothko Foundation, Inc. / 86.3422: 121

Claudio Santini: 31, 32

Photography by Claudio Santini. Reprinted with permission from *Traditional Home*® magazine. ©2001 Meredith Corporation. All rights reserved.: 33

John Singer Sargent (1856–1925). *Madame X (Madame Pierre Gautreau),* 1883–1884. Oil on canvas, 82 1/8 x 43 1/4 in. (208.6 x 109.9 cm). Arthur Hoppock Hearn Fund, 1916 (16.53). The Metropolitan Museum of Art, New York, New York. Image copyright © The Metropolitan Museum of Art. Image source: Art Resource, New York: 122.

Nicolas Sargent: 98, 99

Francis Smith: 5, 102–103, 104, 105, 106, 107, 109, 133, 134, 135, 177, 191, 195 top right, 228

Reprinted with permission from *Traditional Home*® magazine. ©1998, 2004 Meredith Corporation. All rights reserved.: 174, 192

Image © Mogens Trolle, 2012. Used under license from Shutterstock.com.: 70

Evan Joseph Uhlfelder: 165 top, 165 bottom, 168, 169

Jonny Valiant: 2, 6, 179, 180, 181, 182, 183, 184, 185, 186 all, 187, 188, 189

Yale Wagner: 35, 36–37, 38, 39, 40, 41, 42, 43, 44, 45, 46, 49, 51, 52–53, 55 top, 55 bottom, 57 top, 57 bottom, 58, 59 top, 59 bottom, 60–61, 62–63, 64, 65, 66–67, 68, 69 top, 69 bottom, 73, 74–75, 76, 77, 78, 79 top, 79 bottom, 80–81, 82 top, 82 bottom, 83, 84, 85, 86 top, 86 bottom, 87 top, 87 bottom, 88, 89, 90, 91 top, 91 bottom, 139, 140–41, 142–43, 144, 145, 146, 147, 148–49, 150, 151

William Waldron: 131, 132, 136, 137

Roy Wright: 205, 206–7, 208, 209, 210–11

Amanda Zaslow: 163, 164, 166–67, 170–71, 172–73

Library of Congress Control Number: 2012940147

ISBN: 978-1-58093-372-8

10 9 8 7 6 5 4 3 2 1
First edition

Printed in China

Designed by Doug Turshen with Steve Turner

www.monacellipress.com